The Observers Series
HORSES AND PONIES

About the Book

This book provides comprehensive coverage of the breeds of horses to be found throughout the world. There is a full colour illustration and a text description of over 75 famous breeds, and of the other equine species (Ass and Zebra). In addition, all the important breeds are listed under their countries of origin, and brief entries are provided on those not featured in the main text. With a glossary of technical terms, a diagram of the points of the horse, and a full index, the book offers a mass of information, yet in a format ideal to be carried around to shows for quick identification of breeds.

About the Author

Jane Kidd is a well known figure in the equestrian world, with a high reputation as a rider, judge and writer. She has been a member of both the junior and senior British show jumping teams; and has also been an international dressage rider. She is an official judge of dressage, and a member of the Committee for Training and Examinations in Britain. An experienced writer, she is currently a weekly columnist in *Horse and Hound*. She is author of a number of books, including *Festival of Dressage, Horsemanship in Europe, Manual of Horse and Pony*, and compiled for the British Horse Society, *Equitation*. Her particular qualification as author of this book is as author of *Breeds and Breeding*, compiler of *The Complete Horse Encyclopaedia* and as vice-chairman of the British Horse Project, an organization connected with breeding horses.

The *Observer's* series was launched in 1937 with the publication of *The Observer's Book of Birds*. Today, fifty years later, paperback *Observers* continue to offer practical, useful information on a wide range of subjects, and with every book regularly revised by experts, the facts are right up-to-date. Students, amateur enthusiasts and professional organisations alike will find the latest *Observers* invaluable.

'Thick and glossy, briskly informative' – *The Guardian*

'If you are a serious spotter of any of the things the series deals with, the books must be indispensable' – *The Times Educational Supplement*

OBSERVERS

HORSES
AND
PONIES

Jane Kidd

Based on the original book by
R. S. Summerhays

Photographs by Sally Anne Thompson
(Animal Photography)

BLOOMSBURY BOOKS
LONDON

PENGUIN BOOKS

Published by the Penguin Group
Penguin Books Ltd, 27 Wrights Lane, London W8 5TZ, England
Penguin Books USA Inc., 375 Hudson Street, New York, New York 10014, USA
Penguin Books Australia Ltd, Ringwood, Victoria, Australia
Penguin Books Canada Ltd, 2801 John Street, Markham, Ontario, Canada L3R 1B4
Penguin Books (NZ) Ltd, 182–190 Wairau Road, Auckland 10, New Zealand

Penguin Books Ltd, Registered Offices: Harmondsworth, Middlesex, England

First published in hardback format as
The Observer's Book of Horses and Ponies, 1949
Revised editions 1958, 1968, 1978, 1984, 1987

This edition published by Bloomsbury Books, an imprint of
Godfrey Cave Associates, 42 Bloomsbury Street, London, WC1B 3QJ,
under licence from Penguin Books Limited, 1992

3 5 7 9 10 8 6 4 2

Printed and bound in Great Britain by
BPCC Hazells Ltd

Member of BPCC Ltd

ISBN 1-8547-1043-5

CONTENTS

PREFACE

R. S. Summerhays' *The Observer's Book of Horses and Ponies* has been one of the best known reference books for equine breeds for nearly forty years. It has been revised by another breed expert, Daphne Machin Goodall, and it has been my privilege to use their invaluable material as the basis for this new, extensively revised edition. The updating was necessary because mechanization of transport and agriculture have made redundant the work horses which originally formed the majority of the equine population. Their numbers have dwindled, and some breeds have died out. Today's horses are required for pleasure and sport; to meet this demand many new breeds have been developed.

In this new edition over 75 of the world's most famous breeds, arranged in alphabetical order, are covered in detail and illustrated with new colour photographs. A further section comprises a list of all important breeds under their country of origin; those not already featured in the main section are briefly described. The other equine species, the Ass (Donkey) and Zebra are also covered.

It has been my aim to provide comprehensive up to date information about the breeds of the world, yet to preserve as much as possible of the extensive data collected by R. S. Summerhays.

Jane Kidd.

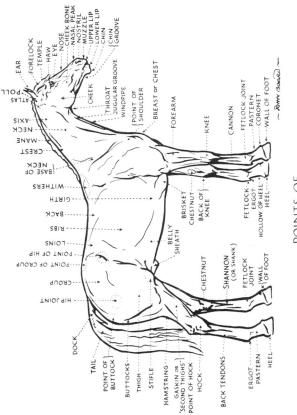

POINTS OF
THE HORSE

EAR
FORELOCK
TEMPLE
HAW
EYE
NOSE
CHEEK BONE
NASAL PEAK
NOSTRIL
MUZZLE
UPPER LIP
LOWER LIP
CHIN
CHIN GROOVE
ATLAS
POLL
CHEEK
THROAT
JUGULAR GROOVE
WINDPIPE
POINT OF SHOULDER
BREAST or CHEST
FOREARM
KNEE
CANNON
AXIS
NECK
MANE
CREST
FETLOCK JOINT
PASTERN
CORONET
WALL OF FOOT
BASE OF NECK
WITHERS
GIRTH
BACK
RIBS
LOINS
POINT OF HIP
POINT OF CROUP
CROUP
HIP JOINT
BRISKET
CHESTNUT
BACK OF KNEE
BELLY
SHEATH
CHESTNUT
SHANNON (OR SHANK)
FETLOCK JOINT
WALL OF FOOT
FETLOCK
ERGOT
HEEL
HOLLOW OF HEEL
HEEL
DOCK
TAIL
POINT OF BUTTOCK
BUTTOCKS
THIGH
STIFLE
HAMSTRING
GASKIN or SECOND THIGHS
POINT OF HOCK
HOCK
BACK TENDONS
ERGOT
PASTERN
HEEL

Akhal-Teké

This, one of the most ancient breeds, was evolved
from the Turkoman (Turkmen), the horses of the
Turkoman tribe in the oases of southern Turk-
menia. It is a close relation to the Iomud from the
USSR and Tchenaran from Iran, and their
ancestors could have been the horses left by the
Mongols who raided and occupied parts of this
territory during the thirteenth and fourteenth
centuries. Owing to the arid desert conditions of
their homelands, the Akhal-Teké horses have from
time immemorial been tethered; their food was not
acquired by grazing, but has been given them by
hand and is a mixture of lucerne and barley.

Today they are still bred in the USSR, in the Republic of Turkmen, but also further afield in Kazakhstan, Uzbekistan, Kirghiz and at the Tersky stud in the northern Caucasus.

Height   They usually stand between 14.2 and 15.2 hands.

Colour   Bays and greys are known, but the most desired is a pale honey-gold with black points. An unusual feature of these Russian horses is that most of their coats have a metallic bloom.

Conformation   Their conformation is elegant, with beautiful heads, a noble expressive eye, a long straight face and long ears. Their necks are long and narrow. The body also tends to be long and the tail low set. The legs are particularly fine and long, with strong bone and high class large feet. There is little hair in the mane and tail. The Akhal-Teké with its narrow frame might be termed the greyhound amongst horses.

Uses   Bred under conditions of great heat and privation, they are resilient and hardy. A group that trekked the 4,000 km (2,500 miles) from Ashkhabad to Moscow in 1935 were without water for three days while crossing a desert. They are also spirited, excellent supple movers, speedy and versatile – all of which has made them high class riding horses. They are fast enough to be used for racing but are best known in competitions, particularly jumping and dressage. The most famous member of the breed was the Akhal-Teké stallion called 'Absent' which won for Russia the Dressage gold medal at the 1960 Olympic Games.

Altér Real

The Altér, like Portugal's other well-known breed of riding horse, the Lusitano, is based on Andalusian stock. Its foundations were laid in 1747, when a court stud was started at Vila de Portel in Alentejo, and three hundred Andalusian mares were imported from the Jerez region in southwest Spain. The progeny were a success, being athletic and intelligent, and they could therefore be used for the then very fashionable high school work, similar to that practised at the Spanish School in Vienna, but by the Altér Real's distant relative the Lipizzaner.

In Napoleonic times, at the beginning of the

nineteenth century, the breed suffered badly. The Vila de Portel stud was sacked during the French invasion of the Peninsular, and subsequently there was considerable outcrossing with foreign and Arabian horses which was said to have spoiled the breed. They were improved again at the beginning of this century when some further Andalusians from the Zapata stud were obtained for cross breeding with the Altér Reals to reinforce the attributes of the original foundation stock.

Since 1932 the Portuguese government has managed the breed and has ensured that only the best horses are selected for breeding stock. The result is that the Altér has been re-established as a breed of high quality, with a worldwide reputation as a particularly athletic riding horse.

Height   15 to 15.3 hands.

Colour   Bay, brown, grey.

Conformation   The general impression is similar to that of the Andalusian. The head is fine with the eyes well apart, the neck is well arched, the shoulder sloping, the body short and deep, the hindquarters muscular and powerful. The legs are particularly hardy with good strong bone.

Uses   These intelligent, spirited horses are very popular for general riding, but are best known as high school animals.

Andalusian

The native Iberian (Spanish) horses were said to
be light, clever and sure footed. When in 711 AD
the Moslems invaded the Peninsula they allegedly
brought with them more than 300,000 horses. A
large number of these were Barbs, which when
bred to the native horses produced the Andalusian.

The name was derived from the province in the
south of Spain where they were originally bred.
Two types were developed: the light Ginete and
the heavier Villanos, the latter coming mainly from
Castile.

The athletic Andalusians were used by the
Spanish court, which did much to promote horse

breeding, both for mounting the cavalry and for high school work and displays, though in the fifteenth century the Neapolitan became a more popular breed of horse for both these purposes.

The Andalusian's greatest promoters turned out to be the Carthusian monks in the monasteries of Jerez de la Frontera, Seville and Castello, who for centuries selectively bred the Andalusian (which thereafter also came to be known as the Carthusian). At the Jerez monastery the monks maintained the breed when elsewhere it was being subjected to cross-breeding and subsequent deterioration. The royal studs were using heavier stallions from Denmark, Holland and Naples for cross-breeding, and in the early nineteenth century many of the finest Andalusians were taken away by Napoleon.

The breed's other promoters were the Zapata family who maintained Andalusian horses at their own stud during these difficult times. Ferdinand VII (1814–33) also gave the breed new support by opening a stud, and since his time they have expanded in numbers and quality.

Height About 16 hands.

Colour Grey.

Conformation Largish head with almost convex profile. The neck strong and well arched. The body close coupled, the hindquarters well rounded, and the legs characterized by short cannon bones.

Uses These intelligent, athletic horses with their elegant high springy action and great presence are well known for their high school work. They are also popular horses for general riding, and even for some harness work, particularly in showing classes.

Anglo-Arab

The Anglo-Arab is so well established that it is
entitled to be considered as a breed despite its
composite nature (Arab and Thoroughbred).

Conditions for registration vary from country to
country, but parents must be Arab and Thoroughbred or Anglo-Arab descendants of such.

In France the Anglo-Arab is the result of such
crossing and of the use of the mares of southwest
France, whose foundation blood dates back to
eighth-century Moorish invasions when stallions
from North Africa were used on the mares of
Aquitaine. The produce was successively known
as Iberian, Navarrine, Bigourdan and Tarbenian.

The Navarrine breed, reminiscent of the Andalusian but of greater size and quality, was almost annihilated in the wars of the Monarchy, the Revolution and the Empire, but under Napoleon I it received a strong oriental influx. Napoleon greatly appreciated Arab horses, and founded two studs, Tarbes and Gélos, where first Andalusian then Syrian horses were used on the native mares. In the 1830s the popularity of the English Thoroughbred led to cross-breeding between it and the Navarrine to produce the taller Bigourdan.

From 1874 selective alternate cross-breeding of native mares with English Thoroughbred and pure-bred Arab produced the Anglo-Arab (or Tarbenian). After 1920 Anglo-Arab stallions were used as a third factor in alternate cross-breeding (English Thoroughbred, Arab and Anglo-Arab).

Height   15.1 to 16 hands.

Colour   Most colours.

Conformation   The French Anglo-Arab has a more consistent appearance than that of other countries, where an offspring may resemble a Thoroughbred, or an Arab, or a mixture. The French horse has a wide forehead, wide-open expressive eyes, longish ears, withers well back, oblique shoulders, a well muscled, well oriented arm, a short well-shaped back, deep chest, and low hocks capable of good engagement. They tend to be light of bone, but have sound strong feet.

Uses   Excellent riding horses, successful in the show ring, and in eventing, show jumping, dressage, endurance-riding and hunting.

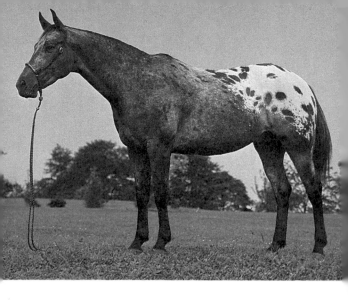

Appaloosa

The spotted horse is featured in many circuses and is used where a striking appearance and a docile temperament are required. It is found in many different parts of the world, but is most common in the United States of America, where commendable efforts have been made to establish and standardize the breed.

The name is derived, it seems, from a breed which was developed by the Nez Percé Indians in the Palouse country of Central Idaho and Eastern Washington, and was produced primarily for war uses.

Something akin to these horses has been found

in ancient Chinese paintings dating back over 3,000 years.

A similar type of horse is known as the Colorado Ranger, and an authority claims that they are American-bred Moroccan Barbs derived from stock imported from Spanish Andalusia.

An infusion of Arab blood has given the horse a touch of quality, which is particularly noticeable in the refinement of head and gaiety of carriage, making it an animal of considerable attraction, not only in appearance but as a riding horse.

Height   14.2 to 15.2 hands.

Colour   The body is pink skinned and covered by a silky white or roan coat with a large number of dark spots superimposed. The spots are of varying size and it is a curious fact that they can be felt by a touch of the finger. They are found on all parts of the body and legs, and are in more profusion on the hindquarters. The effect is very striking. The colouring can vary – the spots often being chocolate rather than black. There is a white sclera around the eye.

Conformation   They are compact in shape, with a short rather straight back. The wither is well defined, the legs are strong and have plenty of bone. The mane and tail are rather wispy. The hoofs are very hard.

Uses   These hard, fast horses are used for a wide range of activities. They are well known as cow ponies, for trail riding, parades, competitions, and gymkhanas, but it is their unusual colour which makes them popular as show animals and in circuses.

Arab

One of the oldest and most beautiful breeds in the world, the Arab, is a descendant of the early horses of central and western Asia. It is thought that wild Arab horses roamed the rough desert lands of the Yemen as long ago as 5000 BC; they may have been first tamed by man around 3000 BC.

The famous promoter of the breed was the Prophet Mohammed, in the 7th century AD. He attached great importance to the horse, and built up the successful cavalry which played a major part in the expansion of the Moslem Empire. Huge numbers of the desert-bred horses were taken on the campaigns through North Africa and into

Spain and parts of France. Many were left behind when the Moslems retreated, and they were bred to local stock to begin the Arab's extraordinary influence on the breeds of the world. Nearly every modern breed is traceable to Arab forefathers.

There are many strains of Arab. There are those of the desert (known as Original or Elite Arabs) with the Bedouin being the breed's most consistent supporters. These nomadic tribesmen needed tough animals to survive the rigours of their climate, but they also prized beauty. They used strict selection in the breeding of their horses: the mares having to prove their courage and stamina in battle and the stallions being chosen for their beauty, conformation and intelligence. Alien blood was prohibited, and some in-breeding led to the prepotency of stamina, soundness and beauty.

Another ancient strain of Arab is the Persian, said to have existed as far back as 2000 BC. It is claimed to be the oldest domesticated breed, and has been maintained in that country to the present day, with occasional additions of desert strains.

The Egyptian Arab is also highly esteemed and dates back thousands of years, for Arab horses were depicted in early Egyptian art. Today some of the most prized are at the El Zahara National Stud and these are mainly descendants of the desert horses collected in the 1850s by Abbas Pasha, viceroy of Egypt.

Of the European strains the Polish Arab is probably the oldest and purest: they were probably brought in as war booty as early as 1560, though most were imported from the Near East by

Polish Arab

enterprising individuals during the nineteenth century. One of the most important of them was Count Wazlaw Rzewuski who captured desert stock of 81 stallions and 33 mares, and established the Sawran stud in 1828. Today the breeding is run by the government, which established a stud at Janow in 1919, and one at Michalow in 1953.

In Germany the important collectors were the kings of Württemberg, whose stud at Weil was founded in 1817. It was handed over to the government in 1932 and today the German Central Arab Stud is at Marbach.

In France the Arab has been influential since the Moslem invasions. Major promoters of the breed were Louis XV, who set up the stud at

Pompadour which is still famous for its Arabs, and then Napoleon who imported much good stock.

Britain became an importer in the late nineteenth and early twentieth centuries, when Wilfred Scawen Blunt and his wife went to Arabia and Egypt and bought some of the best desert material. They returned to start the famous Crabbet stud.

Today the Arab is bred in large numbers in many other countries – the USA and Australia being the most recently established. A World Arabian Horse Organization has been set up to co-ordinate and help breeding around the world.

Height   14.1 to 15 hands.

Colour   Originally bay and chestnut; now grey also.

Conformation   Head small, with concave profile tapering to a very small muzzle. Eyes very large, brilliant, and capable of enormous expansion. Jowl deep and wide. Ears small and sharply cut, quick and pricked. Neck arched and set into the jaws in an arched curve. Withers not high, but sloping into a strong, level back. Chest broad and deep. Hindquarters broad and level. Tail set-on level with the back and carried high. Legs tough; large strong hocks, big flat knees, springy pasterns, well-developed thighs. Feet hard and round. Action free and fast.

Uses   They are used in racing, but only against other Arabs, as although possessing greater stamina they are not so fast as the Thoroughbred. They excel in long distance racing, and are used for general riding and showing. They are still important as an aid in improving other breeds (even the Hanoverian stud keeps Arab stallions).

Ardennes (Ardennais)

The Ardennes horses come from the mountains after which they were named. Their homelands are divided between France and Belgium, and they are called French or Belgian Ardennes according to the region in which they originated. There is also a Swedish Ardennes, produced as a result of the Swedes importing Ardennes into Sweden and crossing them with the North Swedish horse. The progeny are similar but smaller and more agile horses than the foundation stock from the French and Belgian mountains.

The breed is very old and said to be descended from the Great War Horse of the Middle Ages, or even from horses mentioned by Tacitus, and used for military purposes by Julius Caesar. Oriental blood was used to refine it, and in the last three centuries there have been further changes, such as an increase in size and weight by crossing with Brabants. This, however, has led to a loss of power, endurance, vigour and agility.

In the seventeenth century the Ardennes was used as a cavalry horse by Marshal Turenne. During Napoleon's campaign against Russia in 1812 Ardennes horses also distinguished themselves, enduring all the hardships much better than the other cold-blood breeds. This was again the case during World War I, when they worked as artillery wheelers.

There still exists in the mountains a small Ardennes, ranging from 14.2 to 15.1 hands, which is nearest to the old original breed, but the majority are of the heavy draught type.

The Ardennes is a very hardy horse and able to stand up to unfavourable climates and poor feeding. It is still used in France, Belgium and Sweden, but now that transport in towns and work on the farms has become so mechanized, the future of this famous breed, like that of so many other heavy horses, must be uncertain.

Height Around 15.3 hands.

Colour Bay, roan or chestnut.

Conformation Massive, compact body with a very highly crested neck, a broad chest, vast hindquarters and with much feather on the legs.

Uses Agriculture, transport, timber hauling (particularly in Sweden).

Barb

This breed had its native home in Morocco and Algeria. In appearance it is similar to the Arab, but the experts claim that its origins lie with European rather than Asiatic wild stock. It is said, too, to be traceable to a prehistoric African horse. It is by tradition distinguishable from the Arab because of its rather ram-like head, lower set tail, and less gentle temperament.

There are few pure bred Barbs today. Frequent cross-breeding has been practised since the Moslems, mounted on Arabs, invaded Barbary (Morocco, Algeria and Tunis). The Syrian Arab was a particularly popular cross with the Barb, and more recently even European horses have been used.

Several strains of the Barb type can be distinguished. The first group was reared by the Maghrebins on the western side of the plains south of the Atlas Mountains; they called the horse 'Shrubat-ur-rich' (Drinker of the Wind). This horse, which was either grey or brown in colour, was low and greyhound-like in shape. More remarkable is the Bornu breed, from the district south of Lake Chad, which is greyish-white in colour with black legs. A third group occurs typically in the Dongola district of Nubia, and is similar to the Bornu. Smaller horses are known in other areas.

Today some of the best examples of this desert horse of North Africa, which has acted as foundation stock for so many breeds, are to be found at the King of Morocco's Stud.

Height 14 to 15 hands.

Colour Bay, brown, chestnut, black, grey.

Conformation A long head with a straight face. The skull has a sinuous profile similar to that of the Arab. The shoulders are flat, the chest rounded, the hindquarters sloping, with a tail lower-set than that of the Arab. The hair of the mane and tail is profusely developed. The legs are long and strong.

Uses This tough, frugal animal, which can survive on as poor fare as can the Arabian, is a good riding horse. Today, however, it is rarely seen outside its homelands, the Arab surpassing it in popularity.

Boulonnais

The Boulonnais was bred in the northern region of France during the Crusades, and was much improved by Arab and Barb stallions brought from the Levant by the French crusaders. In the course of time the breed was changed – particularly by the admixture of Oriental and Andalusian blood.

Before the railways were established the Boulonnais, a very strong horse with good action and stamina, was used to pull coaches for fast transport such as that needed in the trade to bring fresh oysters from the sea coast to Paris. It enjoyed great fame and was exported to countries where a strong, fast-moving carriage horse with good powers of endurance was needed. In some countries, such as Poland, it was used to improve the local stock.

Today the Boulonnais still has great value, for it is one of the strongest and most impressive draught horses in Europe. It resembles the Percheron both in type and colour. The past infusions of Arab blood are still noticeable in many specimens of the breed and have given it a certain elegance in spite of its massive appearance, a factor which makes it valuable for cross-breeding. It is considered that a dash of Boulonnais blood in 'cold-blood' breeds plays the same role as that of the Thoroughbred in the breeding of saddle horses.

The Boulonnais is bred in two types: the Abbeville, which is of medium size, and the Dunkirk, which is larger and heavier.

Although the breed's name is derived from Boulogne, it is also popular in Picardy, Artois, Haute Normandie and in parts of Flanders.

Height 15.1 to 16.3 hands.

Colour Black, bay, red roan, blue roan and dappled grey.

Conformation Despite being very muscular, heavy and powerful, Boulonnais horses still have an elegant appearance and move with agility. They have a bushy mane and a silky coat.

Uses As very quick maturers they may be used for farm work as early as two years old. At four or five years old they have developed more strength, and can then be used for even heavier draught work. In France they are now used mostly for meat.

Brabant (Belgian Heavy Draught)

Brabant is a low lying region of Belgium, and horses thrive on its fertile soil and succulent herbage. The best known horses reared there are named after the province, and are large, very heavy draught animals with great powers of traction. The famous Flanders Horse of the eleventh to sixteenth centuries lived in the neighbouring region and is said to be the Brabant's ancestor.

In recent centuries there have been relatively few changes to the Brabant and therefore little cross-breeding in its homelands: the result being that it breeds pretty true to type. With its good temperament, willingness to work and its strong constitution it is such a valued performer that it has been exported around the world, both for draught work and for improving other heavy horses. It was used to a great extent for crossing with the now almost extinct Rhenish horse, while those imported to England had a certain influence on our heavy horses. It has also become one of the most popular heavy draught horses in the USA.

Brabants have been bred in Russia – in the Gorki province – both as pure-breds or as stock to upgrade other breeds and types. Some of them are registered in state or district stud books.

Brabants were also used for crossing with the old Belgian mountain breed of Ardennes to increase their size and weight.

Height   15.3 to 16.3 hands.

Colour   Red roan with black points, chestnut.

Conformation   Powerful large horse. The head is rather square, the neck strong and crested, the shoulders and hindquarters massive. The body is close coupled and deep. The legs are relatively short and carry some feather.

Uses   Its strength, weight, presence and good action make it suitable for any heavy draught work which can still be found for horses.

Breton

This French breed is renowned for its great hardiness and working qualities. Bred on the rather poor land of Brittany and exposed to a very rough climate, especially during winter, the Breton makes a very good agricultural horse. It is strong and hardy, and thrives on poor, indifferent food.

There are three distinctive types of Breton, though one of these, the Corlay, is almost extinct. All three are descendants of the indigenous horse of Brittany, but the horses with which they were crossed have turned them into rather different types. The heaviest is the Draught Breton, which has Percheron, Ardennais and Boulonnais ancestors. The Postier Breton is a smaller coach type horse, which has the Norfolk Trotter and Hackney amongst its ancestors. The Corlay, which is rarely seen, is smaller and could be used for riding as well as coach work. It has some Arab and Thoroughbred forefathers.

The Draught Breton is bred on the fertile pastures near the sea coast and represents a type of heavy carthorse. Those from the district of St Pol de Léon, Côtes du Nord and Finistère stand from 15.2 to 16.2 hands, while the Draught version from the southeast of Brest is about 15.2 hands.

The Postier Breton is bred in the interior of Brittany. It is a finer horse, which was lightened by use of English blood. Strong and hardy, it is popular with the farmers.

The existence of these different types and sizes stems from local requirements.

Height   Draught 15 to 16.2 hands; Postier 14.3 to 15.1 hands.

Colour   Red or blue roan, chestnut, bay.

Conformation   Draught short coupled horse, with short well crested neck, short legs and some feather. Postier strong and a very good mover.

Uses   Draught used for heavy work on the farms and in transport. Postier used for coaching and light agricultural work. The ability of the Breton to adapt to different climates and conditions has made it a popular work horse especially in under-developed countries. In France, like other cold-bloods some are used for meat.

Budyonny

The Budyonny is one of the newer breeds in the
Soviet Union. It was developed largely as a result
of the work of a Russian cavalry officer and a leader
of the Revolution, Marshal Budyonny, who after
World War II set out to produce the perfect cavalry
horse. The army stud in the Rostov region of the
USSR was chosen as the base for these activities.
Rigorous, selective breeding was applied, and only
the best progeny was allowed to breed after they
had been thoroughly tested for the required
aptitudes of a cavalry horse, ie, speed, endurance
and character. The most important foundation
stock were the Thoroughbred and Don (usually

Thoroughbred stallions on Don mares), but other Russian breeds such as the Kazakh were also included.

The use of such thorough methods soon resulted in a high class horse and by 1948 the Budyonny had become a recognizable breed, producing true to type and established as a Russian breed. Today they are still bred on the state studs in the Rostov region. They are reared in large herds which run relatively wild in the open lands of that area.

Height 15.2 to 16 hands.

Colour Generally chestnut or bay, and in each can often be found the beautiful golden sheen of so many Russian horses. The Budyonny can also be brown or black.

Conformation This is strong and elegant. The head is well shaped. The neck is crested, the forehand is fine with a well defined wither, the body deep and close-coupled, the hindquarters well developed, and the hind legs powerful. The legs tend to be long and fine, but the bone is dense and the hooves hard.

Uses This intelligent, good-tempered horse is claimed to have considerable speed and athleticism. It is a good mover and although there is relatively little demand for it in its original use as a cavalry horse it has a notable record in steeplechases, eventing, show jumping, and dressage, and is used for general riding. Budyonnys have been victors in the Czechoslovak marathon race at Pardubice.

Camargue (Camarguais)

The grey-white horses of the Camargue inhabit the remote swampland of the Rhône delta in south-eastern France. Their origin, though ancient, has never been definitely established: their shaggy and wild appearance indicates Oriental influence, and it is thought that they could have been descended from the prehistoric horse of Solutré in east-central France. There is no doubt that they have been subjected to crossing, and one of the breeds used must have been the Barb.

Camargue horses still run wild. They breed in free-ranging herds on the poor, reedy pasture which is mostly salty marshland. The uneven, sparse terrain is particularly bleak in winter and searingly hot in summer, and the indigenous horses have to be tough, sure-footed and possess an instinct for survival. Even today man interferes little in their lives except for the occasional round-ups when potential riding horses are caught. These are difficult initially both to catch and to break in, but once the latter is achieved the horses become good, agile mounts, able to jump and even to swim when ridden.

The Camargue was officially recognized as a breed only in 1967. Today local breeders are aided by the Central State Administration. There are about thirty separate herds.

Height   13.1 to 14 hands.

Colour   Whitish-grey.

Conformation   The head is somewhat ugly, with a straight or concave profile. The eyes are placed slightly more to the side of the head than in other breeds. The chest is wide, the barrel large, the rump usually sloping, the limbs strong, with good bone. The mane and tail are full. The coat is rather rough and its general impression gives a hint of primitiveness.

Uses   Agile and strong, these horses are used by the 'Gardiens', the cowboys of the Camargue, to herd the local black bulls which are the region's principal source of wealth, and which are used in the local bullrings (but not killed).

Another source of income for the area is tourism, and visitors enjoy riding round the area on the backs of the tamed Camargue horses.

Caspian

Although only the height of a pony, the Caspian is a miniature version of the horse and has its features. The breed was discovered in northern Iran in 1965, when the American wife of an Iranian saw a stallion of only about 11 hands working in a cart. In subsequent years others of the breed were found grazing along the shore of the Caspian Sea. From then onwards experts have become increasingly interested in Caspians, and from subsequent research it would seem that they are descended from Iran's native wild horse, used by the Mesopotamians in the third millenium BC. In the following centuries, until about the seventh century

AD, this miniature horse is mentioned as being used by the Achmaenians and Sassanians, particularly for ceremonial purposes. It was thought that the breed then became extinct for more than a thousand years; but examination of the bone and blood of the modern version rediscovered in the 1960s has led researchers to argue strongly that the Caspian is related to the ancient miniature horse of Mesopotamia.

The horse's breeding grounds have been between the forested northern slopes of the Elburz mountains and the Persian shores of the Caspian Sea in northern Iran. It is thought that they were brought here from their ancient home of Media by tribesmen from Kermanshah who moved to this area of Iran.

Today a great deal of interest has been focussed on the breed. A herd was built up, and a stud established at the royal stables outside Teheran. Numbers are still very small but some have been exported from Iran, and breed societies such as the one founded in Britain should ensure that these fascinating specimens will survive.

Height 10 to 12 hands.

Colour Grey, brown, bay, chestnut; bay being the most common.

Conformation The head is similar to that of the Arab, with large well-placed eyes, short alert ears, strongly marked jaw, and large low nostrils. The neck is arched, the back short, the ribs well-sprung, the tail set high and well carried, and the hair of both mane and tail fine and silky.

Cleveland Bay

Claimed as the oldest 'established' breed of English horse, the Cleveland Bay is renowned for its stamina, substance, action, wear and tear – with style, fine appearance and good colour.

The breed is of great antiquity, though of uncertain origin. It has long been indigenous in Northern England, chiefly in Yorkshire where it was used for agriculture. While having no hair on its legs, and doing its work very quickly, it was yet able to perform as well as the heavier breeds.

Long famous as a coach horse, it still serves well as a ceremonial carriage horse, the whole bay colouring being suitable and attractive.

Another variation of the Cleveland Bay, the Yorkshire Coach Horse, gained its own identity in the late eighteenth century but today has practically merged again with the Cleveland. It was developed to meet the enormous demand for a bigger, lighter and flashier horse for the more elegant vehicles then appearing in fashionable London. Its basis was the Thoroughbred used with the Cleveland Bay, the original Thoroughbred sires being 'Necromancer' (1816) and 'Servetur'. Use was also made of Arabs and Barbs on the Yorkshire cart mares.

Height   15.2 to 16.1 hands.

Colour   Bay to bay brown. White markings are not desirable, though a small white star on the head is permissible, as are a few grey hairs in heels and coronets.

Conformation   The rather large head, with a convex face, is well carried on a rather long, lean neck. The wide, deep body can be long, but strong with muscular loins. The hindquarters are level, powerful, long and oval, the tail set rather high and springing well away from them. The limbs are strong and muscular. The bone is substantial, the legs clean. The pasterns are sloping.

Uses   It is used for cross-breeding, mainly with the Thoroughbred, to produce hunters and competition horses. The Cleveland Bay is much in demand for driving, and is used in Combined Driving (HRH The Duke of Edinburgh drives a team of Clevelands for the British team), as well as for ceremonial coaching activities.

Clydesdale

The history of Clydesdale Horses dates from the mid eighteenth century, when the hardy native breed found in the then county of Lanarkshire was upgraded to produce a horse with greater weight and substance by crossing it with imported Flemish stallions. This development was effected by local farmers, to meet the demands of commerce created by the rapid growth of the surrounding coalfields. Improved road surfaces caused pack-carrying to be superseded by horse-drawn vehicles, for which larger, stronger horses were needed.

The Clydesdale Horse Society was formed in 1877 and soon published its first Stud Book. Since then a very large number of stallions and mares have been registered. The breed has proved universally popular, and large numbers have been exported.

Clydesdales have quality and weight without grossness and bulk. Active movers for their size, they are thus popular for draught work both in cities and on farms, especially in the north country.

Height Around 16.2 hands.

Colour Bay, brown or black, with much white on face, legs, and often into the body. Chestnuts are rare.

Conformation The feet are round and open. The action varies from the orthodox, as the horse's slight dishing movement – though not exaggerated – means that the inside of the shoe is visible to anyone walking behind. The legs hang straight from shoulder to fetlock joint, with no openness at the knee yet with no tendency to knock. The forelegs are well under the shoulders, not carried bulldog fashion. The hind legs are similar, with the points of the hocks turned inwards rather than outwards, and the pasterns rather long.

The head has an open forehead, broad across the eyes. The front of the face is flat, neither dished nor Roman. The muzzle is wide, the nostrils large, and the eyes bright, clear and intelligent. A well-arched and long neck springs out of an oblique shoulder with high withers. The back should be short, with well-sprung ribs.

Uses All manner of heavy draught work. There is some demand for Clydesdales for cross-breeding to produce heavyweight hunters and riding horses.

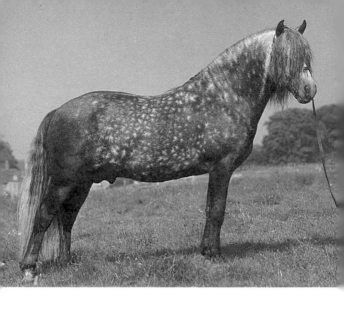

Connemara

The Connemara pony is found in Ireland to the west of Loughs Corrib and Mask, between the Atlantic and Galway Bay. This area has been the home for centuries of an indigenous primitive pony type which until fairly recently was left to fend for itself in wild and hard conditions.

The Connemara Pony Breeders' Society was formed in 1928. It has reduced outcrossing and increased uniformity, with recognized standards, better quality (generally) of mares, and leaving fewer stallions at large on mountain commonages. At the same time the renowned stamina of the breed has been retained.

As with various other primitive European pony breeds, the Connemara's origin is obscure. The unsubstantiated legend is that they originate from horses saved from the wrecks of the Spanish Armada in 1588; but ponies were native to Ireland long before then. It has been suggested that together with the Highland, Shetland, Iceland and Norwegian ponies, they form a Celtic type, but there have been Oriental additions. The breed does have primitive characteristics, but these are combined with signs of an admixture of Spanish and Arab blood. The former could date to the period when Galway merchants traded regularly with Spain. However, the Connemara pony is certainly among the oldest inhabitants of the British Isles.

Height   13 to 14 hands. A height limit of 14.2 hands imposed by the English Connemara Pony Society curbs the breeding of bigger stock.

Colour   Grey, black, bay, brown, dun with occasional roan and chestnut. The predominant colour is grey. Blacks are a little more numerous than browns and bays. The original colour of dun with a dorsal stripe and black points is now very scarce.

Conformation   Intelligent head, crested medium-length neck, well sloped and fine shoulder, compact deep body, strong sloping hindquarters, and short legs. The bone is clean, hard and flat.

Uses   This tough, wiry and typical native pony which thrives on poor keep is bred for itself, and there are many Connemara studs. Intelligent, sound and good tempered, it makes an excellent child's pony. It is also athletic, and is used for competitions, notably show jumping and driving.

Criollo

The Criollo, the native pony of Argentina, is derived from Arab and Barb strains brought to South America by the Spanish Conquistadores in the sixteenth century.

Allegedly the foundation stock was a shipload of cavalry horses which landed in 1535 and were set free soon after the destruction of Buenos Aires by the Indians. They were then driven into the wild environment of the South American pampas where over a period of 300 years rigorous natural selection led to the development of the Criollo. The weak and organically unsound perished, while the survivors became the progenitors of the breed.

Having to contend with such hazards as prairie fires, great changes of temperature, dust storms, frosts and floods, the Criollos became very hardy. Another predominant feature among these wild horses was their dun colouring, similar to that of the sandy wastes, straw, and burnt-up pastures or gravel of the countryside. The Criollo thus benefited from a natural camouflage.

Height   13.3 to 15 hands.

Colour   Dun with dark points, dorsal stripe and dark snippets; also red and blue roan, chestnut, palomino.

Conformation   The head is broad at the base, the poll narrow, the forehead broad but with a narrow face. The neck is of medium size. The withers are clearly defined. The shoulders are strong and sloping. The back is short and deep. The croup is sloping. The forearms and legs are broad, muscular and with good bone. The cannon bones are short, the joints clean and rounded, the pasterns of medium length, the feet small and hard.

Uses   These tough, willing horses with great powers of endurance are used for ranch work and are cross-bred with the Thoroughbred to produce polo ponies. But they are perhaps best known for long-distance riding. The Criollo has figured successfully in many endurance tests: the most famous were 'Mancha' and 'Gato' who, at the ages of 15 and 16, carried Professor A. F. Tschiffely for 21,485 km (13,350 miles) from Buenos Aires to New York.

Brazil's version of the Criollo is the Crioulo, which is about 2 in (5 cm) smaller.

Dales

The Dales have from time immemorial been
natives of the northeast of England. Similar to the
Fell Ponies on the west of the Pennines, the Dales
are today stockier and larger by about 2 in (5 cm).

The Dales Pony, always a weight-carrying type,
was used throughout most of the last century for
carrying lead in convoy from the Northumberland
and Durham mines to the docks. The ponies were
not led, but walked in an orderly fashion, controlled
by a rider. The weight carried on either side of the
body was about 100 kg (16 stone); the weekly
distance covered was about 386 km (240 miles).
They could not have survived such work unless

they were sound and active performers.

Although the working pony has never been so much used for agriculture in England as in continental Europe, the Fell and Dale farmers needed such an animal. With their docility, activity, strength and general hardiness, these ponies have been used extensively for the purpose.

To produce a pony for work on the farms and in transport there was some cross-breeding; the most famous out-crossing was with the Welsh Cob stallion 'Comet', a very fast trotter extensively used on Dale mares in the nineteenth century.

Height 14 to 14.2 hands.

Colour Many are jet black. White markings are rare. Other prevailing colours are bay, brown and occasionally grey; but chestnuts, piebalds and skewbalds never occur.

Conformation The neat and pony-like head has small ears neatly set, with a fine jaw and throat. The neck tends to be short, the shoulders rather steep and straight. The back, loins and hindquarters are high class, being ample, strong and full; the ribs are well-sprung. The tail is not set as high as in some mountain and moorland breeds. There is abundant hair in mane and tail, and much fine hair on the heels. Feet, legs, joints, knees and hocks are all very good. For its size the pony displays great bone, and is of exceptional strength in relation to size.

Uses This sound, hardy pony is easily handled and is used on small farms as well as for pack and trekking work. Today it is popular in the fast-growing sport of driving.

Dartmoor

The rugged waste of Dartmoor, in the extreme southwest of England, with its poor keep, has been for centuries the home of the famous pony of that name. Thus the Dartmoor, in common with the other mountain and moorland breeds of the British Isles, is quite indigenous and quite distinctive, roaming this particularly bleak countryside in a practically wild state.

The ponies remain unhandled unless rounded-up for sale, and few mares and still fewer stallions are ever handled except for branding purposes.

The continuing existence in its natural habitat of the pure Dartmoor has for many years been in serious jeopardy. In the early twentieth century, in order to meet the need for very small pit ponies, certain moormen indiscriminately introduced Shetland stallions to the moors. The result was an indifferent and sometimes degenerate Dartmoor-Shetland cross, which multiplied at the cost of the true Dartmoor. However, the Dartmoor Pony Society has made strenuous efforts to eliminate this regression, introducing stringent upgrading registers. With the help of a few individual breeders, it has managed to safeguard the purity of the breed.

Height Not exceeding 12.2 hands.

Colour Bay, black or brown preferred, but no colour bar except skewbalds and piebalds. Excessive white is discouraged.

Conformation The Dartmoor is a good-looking, compact and elegant pony. Its head should be small, well set-on and blood-like. The ears should be very small and alert. The neck is strong but not too heavy and neither long nor short. The stallions have a moderate crest. The back, loins and hindquarters are strong and well covered with muscle. The feet are tough and well shaped. The tail is set high and is very full, as is the mane.

Uses Dartmoors if handled young make good riding ponies. Although small, they carry a surprising amount of weight. They are also long-lived.

As with all the mountain and moorland breeds of the British Isles, the pure-bred Dartmoor is invaluable as foundation stock for hunters, hacks and children's ponies.

Don

This, once the famous cavalry horse of the dreaded Russian Cossacks, is today a high-class riding horse. It is bred on the steppes around the Don and Volga rivers, where it runs free and has to be tough to survive on rough food and through hard winters. Originally it was a small, hardy but not very pretty horse; but its size was increased and its conformation improved in the nineteenth century, when some of the Oriental based breeds (Turko-man, Karabakh) were turned free with it on the steppes. Later Thoroughbred and Orlov blood were introduced to give it further height and elegance.

The amazing endurance and toughness of these horses was best illustrated by the part that they played in Napoleon's defeat by the Russians. When he retreated from Moscow in the severe winter of 1812 the Cossacks harassed him all the way back to his homeland. There was little food, the weather was atrocious, and many of the French horses died (it is said, as many as 30,000 in one night alone). Yet the Cossacks on their Dons were able to carry out persistent attacks and then to return to Russia: a feat unequalled in cavalry history.

Height 15.1 to 16.0 hands.

Colour Chestnut, bay or grey, but the favourite colour is golden, which is inherited from the Karabakh.

Conformation It has a thoroughbred-like head, with smallish ears and a long, straight neck. The shoulder is often a little upright, and the back straight and broad. The legs are longish; the hindlegs can be sickle-hocked, and all the limbs tend to have the pasterns rather upright. The hooves are large.

Uses Their extraordinary stamina and endurance have made them famed cavalry horses. They are used for general riding, but although energetic their rather restricted action limits their freedom of movement and therefore their potential for competitions. They have also been used to inject stamina into other breeds, acting as foundation stock for the Budyonny and for improving the Kazakh and Kirgiz.

Dutch Draught

The Dutch Draught Horse belongs among the most massively built and most heavily muscled breeds of Europe. Its origins are Belgian, but its immediate ancestors can be traced back to the second half of the last century by means of the Stud Books of the Royal Netherlands Draught Horse Society.

In order to consolidate the characteristics of the breed, since 1925 no horses of unknown pedigree have been entered in its Stud Book; only the progeny of officially registered parents are made eligible for entry. Horses are not entered until their pedigree has been carefully checked and an accurate description has been supplied. When a registered horse is over two and a half years, it may be entered in the Preferential Stud Book, after passing a special examination of its conformation. For an even higher grading of Preferential mares and stallions, inter-provincial prize-winning examinations take place at regular intervals.

Today the breed is recognized as being docile in all circumstances, willing and active, with a pleasant, courageous disposition. It is famous for its exceptionally long working life — it can begin to be used for light work on the farm at two years or even under – for its durability, great fecundity, and excellent breeding performance. It has a quiet and intelligent temperament, and great stamina. It is moderate in its feeding requirements and can be successfully maintained on plain fare.

Height   Up to 16.3 hands.

Colour   Chestnut, bay, grey, black.

Conformation   The Dutch Draught Horse is a massive, hard, deep animal of heavy build. The neck is very short, carrying a not too heavy head. Withers are little developed and shoulders more often than not heavily loaded. The legs are well placed, correctly shaped and heavily muscled, with good feet. The loins are well developed and massive. The back is strong and wide, with well-sprung ribs. The hindquarters are wide, heavy and powerful. The tail is low-set, the croup sloping more perhaps than in any other breed.

Uses   Heavy draught.

Exmoor

The Exmoor, a descendant of the native British wild horse, may have been the pony that pulled the chariots of the Celts. It is believed to be an indigenous animal that has survived in its aboriginal state from earliest times to the present day.

Exmoor covers the extreme west of Somerset and a part of north Devon. It is sparsely inhabited, and the ponies run wild over a series of high bleak moors. Although the 'keep' is of better quality than in the New Forest, the ponies have a hard life in winter. As with the other mountain and moorland breeds, only the fittest survives – stamina and surefootedness being the vital assets.

The true and pure native Exmoor owes much to Sir Thomas Acland (d 1871) and his family, who consistently maintained the old type of pony.

The true-bred ponies roaming the moors remain small, hardy and true to type. Living on grass, and probably never having tasted corn in their lives, yet they carry full-grown men through a long day with the Devon and Somerset Stag Hounds. They have strength, courage, speed and endurance.

Height Stallions not exceeding 12.3 hands; mares 12.2 hands.

Colour Bay, brown or dun with black points, mealy colour on muzzle, round eyes and inside flanks, no white markings.

Conformation Hard, strong, vigorous and alert; the face clean-cut, with wide forehead and short, thick pointed ears. Eyes large, wide and prominent ('toad' eyes), the nostrils wide and the throat clean. The shoulders clean, fine at top and well laid back. The chest deep and wide between and behind forelegs. The ribs are long, deep, well-sprung and wide apart. The back broad and level across loins. The forelegs are straight, well apart and squarely set; the hind legs well apart, nearly perpendicular from hock to fetlock, with point of hock in line with pelvic bone. Action straight and smooth. The coat close, hard and bright in summer.

Uses Large numbers are seen in England, both in harness and as children's riding-ponies. Initially rather wild, they make good and lovable mounts if taken off the moors young enough and handled with care and consideration.

Fell

Fell ponies run wild on the moorlands stretching
west from the crown of the Pennine hills, and in
the mountains of Cumbria. The eastern Pennine
slopes are the home of the related Dales pony.

The origins of the Fell are rather obscure. It is
thought to have a Friesian background: there are
similarities, and some Friesians were brought to
England by the Romans. Another ancestor is
believed to be the now extinct Galloway pony.

Today of all the mountain and moorland breeds,
the Fell seems to breed most true to type. The Fell
Pony Society determinedly guards the purity of its
breed; the cross-breeding that made the once

identical Dale pony larger has been avoided, and alien blood has been shunned.

Fells were used as pack ponies, carrying lead, pannier fashion, 50 kg (8 stone) on each side, from the mines to the docks on Tyneside. They were driven in groups of about twenty, by a mounted man. For centuries they have also been used by the local farmers, for riding, pulling carts, working the farms, and even for sport, such as trotting races.

Height   13 to 14 hands.

Colour   Black is the most usual colour, but bay, brown or grey are known. White markings are rare.

Conformation   A small head with a broad forehead tapering to the nose. The neck of proportional length, giving a good front. The shoulders long and sloping and well laid back. The back strong, the loins muscular. The body short-coupled and deep, with the ribs well rounded. The hindquarters square and strong, with the tail well set. The legs strong, with some feather, but the hair is fine. The pasterns slope but are not too long. The cannon bones are short and there is good bone below the knees. The forelegs can be straight. The hind legs have good thighs, well let down, and clean cut hocks. Mane and tail very full.

Uses   These tough ponies are very active, with high standard paces, a smart true walk and a well-balanced fast trot, showing good knee and hock action and moving well from the shoulder. They are among the best general utility ride and drive ponies, and are used extensively by tourists for trekking holidays.

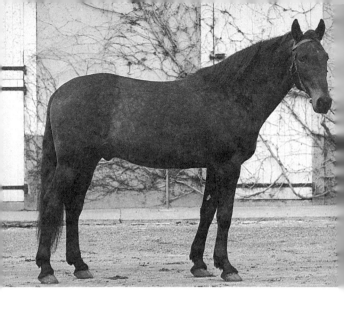

French Trotter

The French Trotter was developed during the
nineteenth century. The sport of trotting started at
Cherbourg in 1836, when a race was held allegedly
in order to find the best horses to put to stud. It
was then gradually taken up throughout the
country. Today about 6,000 trotting races a year
are held in France.

The breed was based on the crossing of native
Norman mares with the Norfolk Trotter stallion
called 'The Norfolk Phenomenon', and the same
type of mares with the Thoroughbred 'The Heir
of Linne'. These were the foundations of the breed,
which was a division of the Anglo-Norman. The

most famous early Trotter stallions were 'Lavater',
'James Watt', 'Phaeton', 'Cherbourg' and especially
'Fuschial' (foaled 1883) who was named the
'patriarche du trotteur français'.

The stud book for French Trotters was started
in 1906. Originally, Anglo-Norman stallions which
could trot 1 km in 1 minute 42 seconds were
eligible for entry.

American Standardbreds were imported into
France to help improve the breed, as were Russian
Trotters, but in 1941 the stud book was closed to
any horse not born of previously registered parents.

The main breeding areas are around the original
studs of Haras du Pin and Haras de Saint-Lô in
Normandy, but there are also studs in the west of
France around Saint Etienne.

Height The French Trotter can stand up to 16.2
hands.

Colour Chestnut, bay, brown. Grey and roan are
rare.

Conformation The type is not standard, but the
impression is of a Thoroughbred type with more
substance. The shoulder is strong and tends to be
rather straight. The body is deep and quite close-
coupled, with a strong back, and sloping hindquarters. The legs are rather long, but very strong.

Uses With their rounded action, which enables
them to trot very fast, they excel at this important
sport. They race both in a sulky and when ridden.
They are also used for cross-breeding, playing a
part in the breeding of the Selle Français.

Friesian

This breed, one of the oldest in Europe, is indigenous to what is now the Netherlands. Today its production is mainly limited to the province of Friesland, where it is bred in the so-called meadow districts and in sandy soil areas.

It has long been popular as an all-round horse for riding, farm and harness work. In the past it was used in warfare, by medieval knights, and certainly by seventeenth-century cavalry leaders, many of whom were painted riding these handsome black horses by the great Dutch artists of the period. It is thought that in medieval times, Andalusian and Oriental blood was added to lighten it; its origins certainly lay with the early cold-bloods. In the nineteenth century its natural energy made it a good basis for Trotters, and it was lightened and speeded up with Trotter stock. As this version was of little use in its principal form of work – on the farms – its numbers declined drastically. Just before World War I it was close to extinction, but judicious crossing with the Oldenburg lead to its revival. During World War II, because of petrol shortages and other factors, it came into its own again. It was honoured in 1954 when Queen Juliana of the Netherlands granted its Breed Society the right to preface its name with the word 'Royal'.

Height   14.3 to 15.3 hands.

Colour   The colour is always black, though a small star is occasionally found.

Conformation   A finely chiselled, longish head with small ears and a shapely neck, with an exceptionally long mane. The back is strong and the ribs deep. The hindquarters are well-rounded. The tail, which, like the mane, carries much hair, is set low. The legs have good bone and are heavily covered with hair, sometimes up to the knee joint.

Uses   Its great 'presence', active manner of going, impressive colour, tractability and natural balanced carriage, make it popular as a circus horse. It is also still used as a utility horse by farmers, but it is perhaps best known as a harness horse. Tjeerd Velstra won a silver medal in the European Driving Championships with a team of Friesians.

Gelderland

This breed of horse derives its name from the Dutch province of Gelderland, where the production is still based. It originated from the native breeds of that area, which in the last century were crossed with a variety of stallions including English Thoroughbreds, Norfolk Trotters, Holsteins, Anglo-Normans and East Friesians. The intention was to produce a horse useful to the local farmers both for agricultural work and as a riding horse.

During this century the main consideration has been consolidation of type, and remarkable results have been achieved in the improvement of the breed. The modern Gelderland is wide and deep, yet of a handsome build with a very stylish action.

More recently, with the growing demand for riding horses rather than farm horses (for which purpose the Gelderland was originally bred), Thoroughbred blood has been added to lighten the breed. The Gelderland has also been used as foundation stock for the Dutch warm-blood which has become one of the most outstanding breeds among competition and riding horses.

Height   Average 15.2 to 16 hands, though larger versions are bred.

Colour   Chestnut, bay or grey.

Conformation   It has a rather plain head, with an almost convex face. The neck is strong and arched, the body compact and powerful. The tail is set high and is also carried high.

Uses   In the past their main use was as farm horses, capable of light agricultural work and of taking their turn at being ridden and driven in harness. Today, with their light active movement and great presence, they are used more for general riding and carriage work. In the Netherlands they are also popular as show horses. Several Royal Studs, including those of Great Britain, were once regular buyers of these horses.

Gotland (Russ)

The Gotland Pony (known locally as the Russ) is claimed to be the oldest breed in Scandinavia, and one that is relatively free from alien blood. Allegedly it has run wild on the Swedish island of Götland since the Stone Age; a herd can still be found there today in the forest of Löjsta, though most are now bred on the mainland.

As with so many other ancient breeds, its ancestry in many respects is open to doubt, though it is thought to be descended from the wild Tarpan, a conjecture strengthened by the dorsal stripe found on many of the ponies. Arab blood was introduced about a century ago, but only in small quantities, and the Gotland has remained comparatively pure bred.

Used in the past mainly on farms and for transport, it lost popularity with the introduction of mechanization. At the beginning of the twentieth century, although the general quality showed a marked improvement, many were exported and the numbers remaining in Sweden were seriously reduced. In the 1950s the Swedish government established a Swedish Pony Association, to foster the numbers and control the breeding. Today successful breeding is taking place.

Height   11 to 12.2 hands.

Colour   Most colours are found, including duns and palominos, but the usual colours are bay or black. They often have a dorsal stripe along their backs.

Conformation   It is a small, rather light and elegant pony, gentle and easily handled. It has a small head with a broad forehead, small pricked ears, big expressive eyes, big nostrils, and a firm mouth. The neck is short and muscular, with long sloping shoulders. The back is on the long side; croup round and short. The legs, though light of bone, are strong and well covered with muscle, while the hooves are small, hard and of good shape.

Uses   Today it is a popular children's pony, capable of particularly good performance over jumps. It is also a very fast trotter, and is used extensively in trotting races which are very popular in Sweden.

Groningen

Essentially a Dutch farm horse, the Groningen
was developed from heavier Friesian native blood,
together with the Oldenburg and East Friesian
(the East German version of the Oldenburg). In
the second half of the nineteenth century local
breeders imported some black Norfolk and Suffolk
stallions. Its principal work in the past was as a
fairly heavyweight farm horse, but there has been
some lightening of the breed to widen its scope of
activities. This has meant that it could be used as a
heavyweight saddle horse, and also as a high class
carriage horse. It has become best known for this
latter type of work, showing speedy, responsive

and stylish action, with much natural bearing and great powers of endurance.

The Groningen's special characteristics are docility and obedience, which make it easy to train and to work, and very popular with its handlers.

The successful development of the Dutch warm-blood since World War II through the crossing of native stock (Groningen and Gelderland) with more refined breeds such as the Thoroughbred, Hanoverian and Selle Français, has meant that the Groningen has a new and important role to play as foundation breeding stock for this successful new breed of competition horse. Sadly, however, with so little demand for it in its own right for its original work on the farm, the Groningen is none-the-less becoming rarer.

Height   15.2 to 16 hands, though larger specimens are found.

Colour   Black, bay brown, dark brown.

Conformation   The face is rather straight and the ears particularly long. The body is deep and powerful, the legs and feet of excellent substance. The tail is set rather high.

Uses   Its ability to thrive on little and poor quality food as well as its docility and strength, made it a popular animal among farmers. Today these qualities, together with its stylish action, ensure its usefulness as a good riding and harness horse. However, its most influential role has been as foundation stock for the world class competition horse, the Dutch warm-blood.

Hackney Horse

The modern Hackney's immediate ancestor is the Norfolk Trotter, or Norfolk Roadster. This energetic well-made animal possessed speed and stamina, and had to be up to weight, often carrying the farmer with his wife riding pillion behind him. The most famous of the breed was the 'Norfolk Cob', bred from 'Fireaway' in the early 1820s. He is recorded as having covered 3.2 km (2 miles) in 5 minutes 4 seconds. Another famous trotter, 'Nonpareil', was driven 160 km (110 miles) in 9 hours 56 minutes 57 seconds. With the advent of the railway, the Norfolk trotter became extinct, but the popularity of the Hackney spread to other parts of England, and overseas to such countries as the USA.

The Hackney has Arab and Thoroughbred blood; almost every Hackney sire can be traced back to the 'Darley Arabian' through his son 'Flying Childers'. Another famous sire was 'Sampson', whose grandson 'Messenger' was the foundation of the American Standardbred trotter.

The Hackney's more remote origins go back to the trotting horse (as distinguished from the ambler and the galloper), which was recorded as early as 1303. There was also at one time a strong infusion of Spanish Andalusian blood.

Height   14.3 to 15.3 hands; can be higher.

Colour   Dark brown, black, bay and chestnut.

Conformation   Small, convex head, small muzzle; large eyes and small ears; longish, thick-set neck; powerful shoulders and low withers; compact body without great depth of chest; tail set and carried high; short legs and strong hocks well let down; well-shaped feet; fine silky coat.

Use   The Hackney today is a pleasure horse used for breeding and showing. Its eye catching paces are shown off when it is driven in the arena. Its shoulder action is free, with a high, ground-covering knee action, the foreleg thrown well forward, not just up and down, with that slight pause of the foot at each stride which gives it its peculiar grace of movement. The hind legs move similarly but a little less freely. At rest the Hackney stands firm and four-square, forelegs straight, hindlegs well back, to cover the maximum ground; the general impression is of alertness.

Hackney Pony

The evolution of the Hackney Pony is somewhat obscure, though in principle it is a smaller edition of the Hackney Horse and shares much of its history.

It is generally believed that the Pony's first appearance was through a 14-hand stallion foaled in the North of England in 1866 and registered as 'Sir George'. It was sired by a horse of the purest Yorkshire blood named 'Sportsman', but nothing is known of the breeding of the dam. From these origins came one of the most spectacular exhibits at English horse shows, and also at those in the USA, where they have been exported. In the USA a Hackney Pony is sometimes referred to as a 'Bantam Hackney'.

Up to the early years of the present century the Pony was widely used by tradesmen for delivery purposes. It was highly prized both as an energetic honest worker, and also as an excellent advertisement because of its flashy appearance and movement.

Height   14.2 hands and under.

Colour   Mostly bays, browns and blacks.

Conformation   The Hackney Pony must be of a true pony type, especially its head. The neck is long, the shoulders good and strong, the body compact and powerful, the limbs hard and the tendons well defined.

Uses   With the decline of harness work the Hackney is now used most extensively in the show ring, where the demand is for the most extravagant action. The fluent action should give a most spectacular effect. The knees should be raised to the extremity and the feet flung forward with rounded action, avoiding any heaviness of forehand. The hocks must be brought right under the body and raised almost to touch it. The whole effect must be arresting and startling, showing extreme brilliance. The best of these ponies fetch high prices both for the home and export trade.

The power of the Hackney's hindlegs gives it great potential as a jumper, but its high-spirited nature makes it difficult for a child to control. Very few pure-breds are thus used as children's ponies, but the cross-breds achieve a certain degree of popularity.

Hafflinger

The Hafflinger Pony is a Tyrolese breed of a small but very sturdy mountain horse, with plenty of bone and a neat head which, when it is climbing, is usually carried close to the ground. Its strength, surefootedness and good movement make it an excellent pack and draught horse, but its true forte is work in the mountains, where it has long been used by the agricultural and forestry industries, as well as by the army.

This eye-catching chestnut pony with its flaxen mane and tail was originally bred in the area of Hafling near Merano in the Italian alps. Legend has it that after the Ostrogoths were finally driven northwards out of Italy in the mid-sixth century, the remnants of them retreated to the Tyrolese valleys around Hafling and when they moved on they left behind them the predecessors of the Hafflinger. It is an accepted fact that there was Oriental blood in the foundation stock, which could well have come from the ponies of the Ostrogoths.

Today the Austrian government promotes the breeding of these ponies on a national scale. In fact the emblem with which they are branded is Austria's national flower the eidelweiss, with an 'H' in the middle.

Height   14 hands.

Colour   Chestnut or palomino, with flaxen mane and tail.

Conformation   They have medium-sized heads with a pointed muzzle. The ears are small, the chest wide, the body deep, the back long and broad. The legs are short and they have a considerable amount of bone.

Uses   With their docile temperament, their frugal nature, their ability to work hard, their sure-footedness and their longevity, they have always been very popular for work in the mountains. Today their uses in agriculture and transport have diminished, but they are used increasingly to take tourists trekking in the mountains and for harness work in the growing sport of driving.

Among the Hafflinger's greatest protagonists were the Germans, who just before World War II provided funds for their breeding as they needed them for transport in the mountains.

Hanoverian

The Hanoverian breed owes much to the influence of Britain's Hanoverian kings, who from the time of George I to the death of William IV in 1837 took a great interest in the horses of their originally native country and sent English Thoroughbreds and Cleveland Bays to cross with the German breeds. In 1735 George II founded the state stud of Celle, still today the centre for the Hanoverian breed, with more than 200 stallions in residence.

The German breed of the eighteenth century originated with the German Great Horse of the Middle Ages, described as follows by the sixteenth-century writer Thomas Blundeville:

74

The Almaine is commonlie a great horse, and though
not finelie, yet verie stronglie made, and therefore more
meete for the shocke than to pass a cariere, or to make a
swift manage, because they are very grosse and heavie
... The desposition of this Horse (his heavy mould
considered) is not evill, for he is verie tractable, and will
labour indiffirentlie by the way, but his pace for the most
part is a verie hard trot.

With the disappearance of armour the horse had
to be modified to produce a finer and more agile
mount. In the seventeenth and eighteenth centuries first Holstein blood was used, then some
English, followed by Neapolitan, Andalusian and
Prussian. By the end of the eighteenth century
little outside blood was used to produce this horse
for carriage, army, and farm work. It was a fairly
hefty, strong animal with a rather plain head,
straight shoulder and flat hindquarters with tail
high-set.

Since World War II, with the growing demand
for competition horses, the Hanoverian Breed
Society has been far-sighted enough to add Thoroughbred, Trakehner and Arab blood in order to
refine the carriage horse.

Height   15.3 to 17 hands.

Colour   All solid colours.

Conformation   Plainish head, strong neck, deep
body, strong hindquarters.

Uses   Their powerful, extravagant action and
sensible temperament have placed them as the
most popular breed of competition horse in the
world. Today Hanoverians excel in show jumping,
dressage, and (when they have enough Thoroughbred blood) eventing.

Highland

The homelands of Britain's largest and strongest mountain and moorland pony are the Highlands of Scotland and certain adjacent islands.

The Highland pony is of great antiquity. It is said that after the Ice Age in Europe ponies from northern Asia moved westwards, the larger ones (now represented by the Scandinavian and Highland ponies) keeping to the north, and the smaller (Eastern breeds) making for the south.

In the past there were two versions of the Highland pony. The smaller, finer one was known as the Western Isles, and not long ago these ponies, from such islands as Barra, stood no higher than a

Shetland. The larger and stouter Garron, or Mainland Pony (thought to be the modern version), was developed in the last century to meet the demand for stronger ponies in forests and on farms. Today cross breeding has led to the end of any distinction between the Western Isles and Garron.

Highland ponies have had an infusion of alien blood, mostly Arabian.

Height   13 to 14.2 hands.

Colour   Black, brown, chestnut with silver mane and tail, varying dun or grey with no white markings. An eel stripe along the back is typical, but not always present.

Conformation   Head attractive and broad, eyes bright and prominent; nostrils wide. Ears short. In profile the breadth, rather than the length, of the head and jawbone should be pronounced. Neck, strong, crest arched, with flowing mane. Shoulders set back; withers not too pronounced. Back short, with slight curve; chest deep; ribs deep. Hindquarters and loins powerful, thighs short and strong. Tail has plentiful hair. Legs flat in the bone, with a fringe of straight silken feather ending in a prominent tuft at the fetlock joint. Forelegs placed well under the body. Pasterns oblique, not too short. Hooves broad and firm. Action free and straight.

Uses   The stronger Highlands are used for deer stalking and for farm work. They are first-class for hill work, because of their surefootedness and good balance. Finer Highlands are popular as children's ponies. All types are used for trekking.

Holstein

The Holstein is another very good German breed, suitable for both riding and driving. Its origins are thought to date back to the thirteenth century, and in the Middle Ages it was used as a warhorse. It was bred on very good pastures of alluvial origin on the right bank of the River Elbe, in Schleswig-Holstein. In the sixteenth to eighteenth centuries the breed was very highly esteemed both at home and abroad, and was exported to many countries, notably France. Just before World War II there was a great demand for it in South America and elsewhere, while in Germany it was mostly used as an artillery horse.

The first famous stud for Holsteins was the Royal Stud at Esserom. After Schleswig-Holstein was annexed to Prussia the Traventhal Stud was founded, and when this closed in 1960 the centre for the breed became the Elmshorn School in Schleswig-Holstein.

According to E. Iverson's *Abstracts of Animal Breeding* (1939) 'Das Holsteiner Pferd, 1937':

'From 1825 onwards a reorientation of breeding took place, particularly owing to the introduction of the Yorkshire Coach Horse. The resulting compact conformation, combined with a satisfactory gait, proved successful, and an increased demand for Holstein horses again caused a serious dearth of breeding of uniform quality. This led to the organization of breeders and of the central stud at Traventhal. Contrary to the usual policy in German 'warm-blood' breeding, the English Thoroughbred influence in Holstein is negligible, but half-bred stallions contributed to the present excellence of the blood.'

Since World War 2 however English Thoroughbred blood has been used with great success to turn it into a more refined top class competition horse.

Height   Usually over 16 hands.

Colour   Normally brown, bay or black.

Conformation   The Holstein horse is a very fine, strong animal with good legs, free action, good gaits and endurance.

Uses   Over the last decade the Holstein has been turned into one of the world's best competition horses, winning Olympic medals in dressage, show jumping and horse trials.

Hungarian Half-bred

Hungary is renowned for its horse breeding. In the last century English Thoroughbreds were imported and at the state-owned Kisber stud such excellent versions were bred that they were able to win many international races. The most famous stallion 'Kisber', named after the stud where he was bred, won the 1876 British Derby.

Half-breds were also produced extensively and successfully for use by the cavalry and for light agricultural work. Today these half-breds are produced at the various state studs for general riding and sports, but they are most famous as driving horses.

The breeds developed in the nineteenth century were named after their foundation sire, which was put to the local mares and in some cases like the Furioso and Gidran also to Arab stock. 'Gidran' was an Arab and he founded an Anglo-Arab type breed. 'Nonius' was an Anglo-Norman and his stock were heavier all-purpose animals. 'Furioso' and 'North Star' were Thoroughbreds imported from England in the mid-nineteenth century.

Today the Gidran is still maintained as the Hungarian Anglo-Arab but the Furioso and North Star have been merged to start the officially designated main breed of Hungarian sports horse, the Mezohegyes, produced at the stud after which it is named. Some Hanoverians and Holsteins have also been used to improve this new Hungarian Half-bred.

A lighter Hungarian Half-bred is the Kisber, again produced at the stud after which it was named. This has more Thoroughbred in it. The most famous Half-bred however comes from the Kecskemet stud where Trotters (originally imported from Russia and America) are crossed with Lipizzaners to produce world class driving horses.

Height 15.2 to 16.2 hands.

Colour Most.

Conformation Sound riding horse types ranging from the lighter Kisber to the heavier Mezohegyes.

Uses The Kisber has enough stamina and 'class' to be an eventer, the Mezohegyes is a good general riding and competition horse, but it is the smaller Half-bred based on Lipizzaner stock which is most famous as a driving horse.

Icelandic Pony

The ponies of Iceland are not indigenous but are immigrants, like the human inhabitants with whom they came from Norway, Orkney, Shetland and the Western Isles in the ninth century. The present animal is a mixture of two early varieties of the Celtic types.

The Norse settlers used their ponies for both domestic purposes and for horse fighting. They also ate horse flesh at feast times, until their conversion to Christianity at the end of the tenth century.

Today, Icelandic ponies are usually graded into riding, pack, and (to a lesser extent) draught, though the latter are also ridable. The riding ponies are broken to an ambling gait which is comfortable and fast for long distances. For the thousand or so years of their history they have been the only means of transport in Iceland.

Attempts to produce a finer, more breedy type of Thoroughbred-cross as a suitable pony for children have failed – the best characteristic of both strains having been lost. The Icelandic pony seems to be a mixture rather than a breed and will not breed true outside its own blood.

Until recent times there was a steady trade in England for the Icelandic pony, many going to work in the pits, others finding themselves between the shafts, mostly in the towns.

Height   12 to 13 hands.

Colour   Most colours but usually grey or dun.

Conformation   Short and stocky, with large heads and intelligent eyes, very short, thick necks, and heavy mane and forelock.

Uses   They are hardy and have keen sight. They also have a pronounced homing instinct, and the customary way of returning a pony after a long trek is to turn it loose: it will usually find its way home within 24 hours. Not much ordinary horse training or horsemastership is possible with them, and the usual method of control is by voice. In character they are docile and friendly, although like all small pony breeds they are sturdily independent by nature. These characteristics make them well-suited to help the islanders on the farms, and as a means of transport.

(There is a similar type, the Faroe Islands pony.)

Irish Draught

The Irish Draught evolved from the adapting of
native horses to make them suitable for work on
small farms. They did not need the strength of
cold-bloods, the Irish farmer wanting a utility
horse that he could put in harness, drive and ride.
The original Irish Draughts were the produce of
imported Thoroughbred sires in the eighteenth
and early nineteenth centuries and the stronger
Irish mares, many of which already had an infusion
of Spanish or Arabian blood.

During the nineteenth century the Irish
Draught was popular among farmers and land-
owners for farm work and hunting, but the

agricultural recession of 1879 led to a decline in numbers. When the economy improved again, farmers had to import Clydesdales and Shires. These were cross-bred with the remaining Irish stock, resulting in an increase of feather and coarseness amongst the Irish horses.

At the beginning of the twentieth century the government in Ireland introduced Registration Schemes: in 1907 for stallions, in 1911 for mares, and inspections were held. World War I provoked further interest in the breed because of their value to the army, and in 1917 an Irish Draught Stud Book was introduced.

As its use on the farms declined, the Irish Draught was used more and more for cross-breeding, to produce the hunter and then the show jumper. This resulted in the diminution of the foundation stock, but with the formation of the Irish Horse Board in the 1970s, steps have been taken to ensure the continuance of the breed. There is now a good nucleus of Irish Draught.

Height 15 to 17 hands.

Colour Bay, brown, chestnut, grey.

Conformation The face is rather straight, the neck is short and thick. The body tends to be long, and the hindquarters slope sharply but are very powerful. The bone is good and flat. There is very little feather on the legs. The forelegs tend to be rather straight. The feet are large and round.

Uses This active, courageous, sound horse is a good heavyweight hunter and versatile farm horse. But its main use is to cross-breed with the Thoroughbred to produce competition and riding horses.

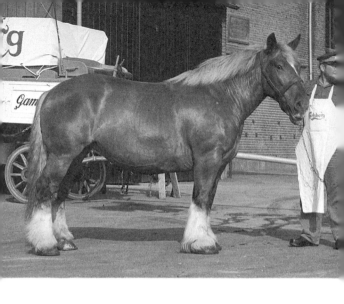

Jutland

As the name suggests, this breed originated in Jutland, where it is still produced. Its value as a draught horse was realised at a very early date and some were taken from Jutland to the Danish islands. It is a very old breed, said to date back to the Viking period, around 800 AD. In the ninth and tenth centuries when the Danish settlers came to Britain they brought with them horses of the Jutland type. The similarity between the Jutland and the Suffolk Punch from England indicates that some of the former must have acted as foundation stock.

The Jutland type was also used as the Danish

War Horse during the Middle Ages. It was strong and agile, and was an ideal mount for the heavily armoured knights when going into battle.

British horses played a part in the adjustment of the Danish breed of heavy horses – mainly in the nineteenth century when Yorkshire Coach horses and Cleveland Bays as well as some of the Jutland's close relations, Suffolk Punches, were imported to lighten it. The most influential was the Suffolk stallion 'Oppenheim LXII', imported into Denmark in 1860 and thought to be a Suffolk/Shire crossbred. He became the ancestor of some of the best stallion lines, within which were 'Aldrup Munkedal'. 'Hövding', 'Fjandbo', 'Skjalden', 'Lune Dux', 'Hof' and 'Himmerland Eg'.

The Danes have a long tradition of horse breeding, and they have been particularly skilful and consistent in their methods of selective breeding which have improved the Jutland to a very high level. In its turn the breed has been used to improve other countries' cold-bloods and to act as foundation stock.

Height 15.2 to 16 hands.

Colour Predominantly chestnut, but sorrel and roan are also found.

Conformation This is a massive horse for its medium size, with a very broad deep body and short legs. The head is plain, the ears long, the neck short. The legs have tremendous bone, with soft smooth hair.

Uses Its excellent temperament and strength have made it a popular draught animal long used on Danish farms and for transport purposes.

Kladruber

The Kladruber derives its name from the stud where it was developed at Kladruby-on-Elbe, which now lies in Czechoslovakia. This is the oldest operating stud in the world, founded in the sixteenth century by the Emperor Maximilian II when he imported Spanish horses of Andalusian type to this part of Bohemia. Close by is the racetrack of Pardubice where the famous annual steeplechase is staged.

The early occupants of the stud were the ancestors of the Kladruber, a breed developed from crossing Barbs and Turks with the heavy native horses of the Alps. It seems that little other blood was added except some from Lipizza (which were Lipizzaners of the same origin). It is also thought that a few came from Hungary. The Kladruber developed an appearance which was very similar to but rather larger than that of the Andalusian.

As a result of the upheavals of World War II in that area, the breed was neglected and almost died out; but when peace came efforts were made to restore numbers and to give the breed a little more substance by importing some outside blood. The breeds selected were some of the best known Western European warm-bloods – Oldenburgs, Anglo-Normans and Hanoverians.

The Kladrubers' main use has been as coach horses, and for a period they were used by the Imperial court in Vienna. Until the early nineteenth century not only grey but also black horses (later kept separately, at Slatjiniany) were bred at Kladruby, and a black team was used for the funeral of Emperor Franz Josef in November 1916. Today they are a spectacular attraction at international events, the Kladruber stud presenting teams of up to 16 horses – all of them grey – pulling one carriage.

Height   16 to 17.1 hands.

Colour   Grey.

Conformation   They have a noble, well-proportioned stature. Though very similar to the Andalusian and Lipizzaner, they have more height and substance.

Uses   Their intelligent, kind character and strength has made them best known as carriage horses, but they are also used for work on farms.

Knabstrup

This is an old Danish breed consisting of picturesquely spotted horses. The spots usually conform to patterns known as 'leopard', 'snow-flake' and 'blanket' (these are some of the Appaloosa patterns).

During the Napoleonic Wars, Spanish troops were stationed in Denmark for a short period, and one of their officers left behind a spotted mare, which although relegated to the honest work required by a butcher in the delivery of meat, proved outstanding both in speed and endurance. Major Villars Lunn, the owner of an estate known as Knabstrup, subsequently bought this chestnut mare, which had 'blanket' markings with a white

90

mane and tail and was of English hunter rather than of Spanish type. Both the Major and his father before him were great breeders of horses of riding type, always laying special stress on hardiness, speed and endurance; their stock originated from the famous Royal Fredericksborg Stud where Spanish-Arab-Barb types known as Frederiksborgs were bred.

The butcher's mare, which was named 'Flaebehoppen', became the foundation mare of the Knabstrup breed. In 1812 she was put to a Frederiksborg stallion of Palomino colour and produced a colt 'Flaebehingsten'. He became the foundation stallion of the breed. Though similar in marking to the original mare, he had colourings of lighter shades, giving a rather peculiar metallic appearance, and he was described as having 'more than twenty colours'.

There has been a good deal of cross-breeding recently, in an effort to produce better patterns of spots, but with little regard to type. This has resulted in a great variety of horses, inconsistent with the establishment of a breed.

Height Around 15.3 hands.

Colour Appaloosa patterns on a roan base.

Conformation Varies, but stocky, well-made horses.

Uses With the inevitable variations which occur in all spotted markings, the Knabstrup is sought as a circus horse. It is used, too, for general riding.

Konik and Huçul

These tough, robust Polish ponies are mainly descendants of the wild horses of that eastern area of Europe – the Tarpans. The Steppe Tarpan was said to have been the ancestor of the Konik. The name means 'small horse', and although of pony height the Koniks have the features of horses. They have provided foundation stock for many of the pony and horse breeds of Eastern Europe, particularly Poland and west Russia.

With its Tarpan base the Konik is resilient and frugal, yet, as it combines those qualities with a kind, tractable nature, it is an excellent work pony for the lowland farmers of its homeland, which is mainly east of the river San.

The mountain version of the Konik is known as the Huçul, whose homeland is the Carpathian mountains. Although sometimes referred to as the 'Forest Tarpan', today's version is not derived from pure Tarpan stock as a good deal of Arab blood has been introduced.

The Huçul is smaller than the Konik and is particularly surefooted. It is used extensively for pack work in the mountains and for agricultural activities on the hill farms.

The Huçul's second name is derived from its area of origin, as it is often called the Carpathian pony.

Both these breeds of Polish ponies are bred by farmers and on state studs at Popielmo and Jezewice. Selective breeding of the Huçul now takes place at Siary near Gôrlice. They still receive government aid for breeding as they play a part in the country's economy, being used as work ponies in much of Poland.

Height Huçul 12.1 to 13.1 hands; Konik 13.1 hands.

Colour A variety of dun colours, but usually showing the dorsal stripe.

Conformation Strong, good conformation, but tendency to have cow hocks. The head is long and broad like that of the Tarpan.

Uses These ponies are tough and easy to train. They can survive on little food and enjoy a very long life. They are used mainly for general work on farms.

Latvian

The Latvian breed was developed in what is now
the Baltic state of Latvia, USSR, but it was not
finally established until 1952. Before that time it
had been subjected to many changes. Its origins
are ancient, and it is thought to have been an
example of the forest cold-blood of northern
Europe. The native cold-blood types have, during
the last three centuries at least, been crossed with
various lighter breeds to make it into a more agile,
heavy, all-purpose horse. Recently the breeds used
have been various German warm-bloods (Hanoverian), Arabs and some Thoroughbreds.

Until this century the Latvians were heavier,

94

and were used mainly for draught work and transport. Today, with the continued lightening of the breed, they are a general purpose harness horse, used on farms, for city transport, and as heavy-weight competition and riding horses.

There are three types of Latvians. The basic type is the most common and includes more than three-quarters of the breed; it is a tough well-made type with plenty of bone and substance. The harness type is taller. The lighter type is the Latvian Riding Horse which is developing from the harness type and Hanoverians, Arabs and Thoroughbreds.

Height   15.2 to 16 hands.

Colour   Bay, dark brown, black and chestnut are the most common.

Conformation   It has a large head, with a straight face and big eyes. The neck is strong and arched, the body powerful, rather thickset, deep and broad. The hindquarters are strong and muscular. The legs are tough, and there can be a little feather on the heels. There is plenty of hair in the mane and tail.

Uses.   They are Russia's all-purpose breed. In the south they carry out mainly draught work, whereas in the north they work under saddle as well as harness. They are popular with farmers, and are also ridden extensively. They have great powers of endurance and are very strong. It is common practice to put them through endurance and pulling tests before breeding stock can be used at stud.

Lipizzaner

This famous Austrian horse has Spanish origins. Its ancestors were bred by the Moors who crossed Berber, Arab and Vilanos horses (from the Pyrenees). The produce were intelligent and athletic, and in 1580 Archduke Charles imported 9 stallions and 24 mares, stabling them at the stud of Lipizza which is now part of northwest Yugoslavia.

The resulting animals showed exceptional ability at the high school work which was in vogue in the courts of Europe during the sixteenth, seventeenth and eighteenth centuries. More horses of the same types were imported from Spain. These and their produce were used in the Spanish Riding

School at Vienna, after its inauguration in 1735.

For 350 years Lipizzaners were bred at Lipizza, but after World War I it became part of Italy. As the horses' new home, the Austrians chose Piber, in the south. Traditionally there have only been a limited number of breeding horses, and at Piber today there are between 130 and 150. To avoid the ill effects of too much in-breeding, outside blood has been occasionally introduced, including German and Danish stock. (In the nineteenth century Arabians had been introduced.)

Breeding has always been strictly selective, the guiding principle being performance. Only stallions which have proved to be outstanding performers at the Spanish Riding School are used to reproduce the Lipizzaner. The mares, too, have to go through performance tests at the stud.

Height 15 to 16 hands.

Colour Born dark, they usually go grey by the age of seven, although the odd bay is found.

Conformation The Lipizzaner is shapely and elegant in appearance, with a longish body, well ribbed up, strong hindquarters, a well crested neck, and a small head with legs which have plenty of bone. The nostrils are rather narrow, the eyes large and horizontal. The general impression is of strength, grace and dignity.

Uses These intelligent, docile but athletic animals are renowned for their high school work at the Spanish Riding School. They obtain great collection and perform 'airs above the ground'. They are also bred in Yugoslavia and Hungary, where they and their crossbreds are used for harness work.

Lusitano

This is a Portuguese breed of horse well known for its exploits in the bull ring. Its origins are rather obscure, but all Portuguese breeds are closely related to the Spanish, the horses found in the Iberian peninsula having been influenced by the stock that the Moors brought with them in the seventh century AD. They were of Arab and Barb blood, from the desert.

It was in the twelfth century that Portugal separated from Spain and established itself as a kingdom. Eventually its horses became distinguishable from the Spanish, the latter being represented by the Andalusian and the Portuguese

98

by the Altér and Lusitano. The Lusitano is thus very similar to the Andalusian, but is thought to have a little more Arab in it.

In the past the Portuguese used the Lusitano mainly for military purposes, but as it is a strong breed it has been very popular for farm work and is still used in small numbers on the farms.

Height   15 to 15.3 hands.

Colour   Grey is most common, but other solid colours are found.

Conformation   The general appearance is similar to that of the Andalusian. The face is rather straight, the ears small but reactive. The neck is strong and the shoulder is good, with a distinct slope to it. The body is compact and deep. The hindquarters are very powerful. The mane and tail have an abundance of hair, which tends to be wavy.

Uses   The Lusitano is a very courageous, athletic and intelligent horse, which has proved to be easily trainable. Though Lusitanos are still used for light farm work, their present fame is due to their connection with the mounted bullfighters of Portugal (*rejoneadores*) who train them to performances of high school standard in the bull ring. Some perform before the bull appears, when they demonstrate many of the spectacular movements of advanced dressage. Others, schooled to an equally high standard but with a superior turn of speed, are used during the actual bull fight. Only horses with great athleticism and courage can fulfil these functions, hence the Lusitano's fame. These assets also make them popular as high school horses.

Mongolian Wild Horse (Przevalski's Horse or Asian Wild Horse)

Ancient cave drawings of animals familiar to prehistoric man were found in Spain and France in the nineteenth century. One animal depicted was a small pony-like creature with a large head, a rather Roman nose and a tufted tail. It is very similar to Przevalski's Horse.

In 1881 the skin and skull of a prehistoric horse were obtained by the Russian explorer Colonel N. M. Przevalski, after whom it was named *Equus przevalskii przevalskii* Poliakoff. It has been described as intermediate in character between the horse and the Kiang strain of onager. An expedition sent to the Gobi Desert in 1902 captured 32 foals. From these, two colts eventually reached the London Zoo, which jointly with Whipsnade and Marwell now possesses a small herd.

Height   About 12 hands.

Colour   Dun with a mealy muzzle, a dark stripe on the back; some black below the knees and hocks. The mane is erect in summer, but in winter, when the coat is long and thick, tends to fall over.

Conformation   A massive head with short ears, small eyes set relatively high, heavy jaws and unusually big teeth. A stocky body, with heavy neck and straight shoulders. The tail has a terminal tuft; the hairs at the root are rather harsh. Legs fairly slender, pasterns well sloped.

Uses   In 1981 there were around 350 specimens in captivity; the largest herd is in Prague Zoo. Efforts are now being made to re-establish wild herds in Mongolia.

Its closest relation is the Mongolian, once thought to be the domesticated version. It now seems that more strains were involved. These ponies are widely bred by various Mongolian tribes, and are exported to China for racing and polo, and to produce the China Pony. They have mingled with Arabians to produce Turkomans, and have influenced Spitia, Bhutia, and Manipur ponies.

Height   12.2 to 13.3 hands.

Colour   Black, bay, dun.

Conformation   Heavy head and shoulders, small-lish eyes, thick neck, deep chest, well sprung ribs, good hindquarters, loins and legs, plenty of bone.

Uses   They are working ponies of nomadic tribes.

Morgan

The Morgan breed was founded in the 1790s in Massachusetts by a single stallion originally called 'Figure'. In 1795 he was acquired by a Vermont innkeeper named Thomas Justin Morgan in settlement of a bad debt. The horse was renamed after his new owner and taken to Vermont, but Morgan soon died and the horse was passed on to various new owners until he came into the hands of a farmer named Levi Bean.

Bean was a hard taskmaster and worked the horse, which stood between 14 and 15 hands, in all manner of ways, making him plough, move timber, and help with other farm work. During holidays he was entered in races, both harness and saddle, and was said to have been unbeaten in weight-pulling contests. This tough horse also served a large number of mares and showed tremendous prepotency, with all his foals inheriting his physique and unusual all-round ability.

There is no record of the stallion's origins, but his appearance indicates Welsh Cob with a mixture of Thoroughbred and Arab. This hard working animal died when he was well into his twenties, leaving behind him a progeny that ensured his fame. He had finally been acquired by the US Army, and was established at stud in Woodstock, Vermont.

Morgans are great all-round horses. They work under saddle, as well as in harness, where they have shown tremendous pulling power for their size. They are also capable of high speed as roadsters (a form of harness racing). By far the largest number of them is found in their country of origin, the USA, where they are used for competitions and showing classes when ridden or driven. Quite a number have also been exported.

Height 14 to 15 hands.

Colour Any solid colour, but chestnut is most common.

Conformation The head is small, the shoulders strong. The back is short and muscular and the hindquarters are rounded and big. The legs are fine and strong. It is a compact muscular horse.

Uses These strong versatile horses are used in harness and for riding, and are popular today in the show ring.

Mustang

The term 'Mustang' was applied primarily to the feral or semi-feral horse of the plains of western North America, but has been extended to include the herds on the pampas of South America.

The American horse is itself of Spanish origin: the animals that Cortes took over from Cuba in 1519 being the first true horses seen in the New World. Without the horse Cortes could not have conquered Mexico, nor Pizarro, later, Peru. A complete list which exists of the horses of Cortes indicates that they were of Spanish blood, going back to Saracen (Arabian and Barb) ancestry.

During the mixed adventures of the Spanish

conquerors, many of their horses strayed or were captured by the Indians, and from them sprang the vast herds of feral horses that roamed the Great Plains in early American pioneering times. These horses – which enabled the American Indian to become the superb natural horseman that he was and still is – multiplied considerably in the three succeeding centuries. To all of them the comprehensive name of Mustang was given, but there were various types such as the Chickasaw horses in the south-east, and the Bronco and Cayuse which were further north than the original Mustangs of California, Texas and New Mexico.

Today the true Mustang has been largely succeeded by the various American breeds – Quarter Horse, Appaloosa, Pinto and Palomino, all of which number Mustangs among their foundation stock.

Height The original Mustang was a small horse, seldom more than 14.2 hands.

Colour Every known colour was represented, with many strange shades and combinations.

Conformation Sturdy, wiry frame. Good bone and hard legs; scraggy, rough, of uncertain temper, but hardy and courageous. Occasional throwbacks to their remote Arabian ancestry were known.

Uses Once broken and domesticated, the Mustang is a useful light saddle-horse, and was the original cow pony.

Wild Mustangs came close to extinction before a law was passed to protect them by establishing areas where they can roam. They played a romantic part in the history of the American West.

New Forest

The New Forest Pony is – apart from the Highland – the largest of the nine mountain and
moorland breeds of the British Isles. Its ancestry is
uncertain. Wild horses were mentioned as living
in the Forest in Canute's reign, and there can be
no doubt that they have been there ever since.

The breed has been subject to a considerable
amount of 'improving' by various infusions. In
1852 Queen Victoria loaned an Arab stallion,
'Zorah', which was in the Forest for eight years.
During this century no alien stallions have been
turned loose and the pony has become a definite
type, increasingly breeding true to it.

Today the New Forest Pony roams at will over some 24,280 hectares (60,000 acres) of countryside in Hampshire, but the land is mostly bare of trees and offers the poorest pasture to the ponies, consisting in the main of heather and poor or rank grass. This has caused them to be hardy and economical feeders.

New Forest Ponies play an important part as foundation stock. Bred to survive the constant struggle for existence, they develop acute intelligence, courage and resourcefulness. They are adept at picking their way over rough ground and are very surefooted. Accustomed to seeing many tourists in the New Forest, they are less shy of mankind than other mountain and moorland breeds; they have also become immune to every kind of road terror and thus make the safest possible mounts for children when properly broken-in.

Height   There are two sizes: Type A up to 13.2 hands; Type B 13.2 to 14.2 hands.

Colour   Any except piebald or skewbald.

Conformation   The head is well set on and the neck a little short from throat to chest, but the good, laid-back shoulder gives plenty of length of rein. The back is short and the loins and hindquarters strong. The forearm and second thigh are good, the cannon bones are short and the feet good. The pony should have plenty of bone and its action should be straight but not exaggerated.

Uses   General riding – Type A is suitable for children. Type B, with its extra height, bone and substance, is strong enough to carry adults.

Norwegian-Fjord

This attractive pony is among the most distinctive and interesting breeds of Europe. Two types are recognized: the *fjord-hest* of western Norway and the *doele-hest* or 'valley horse' of the interior. Their characteristics are the same, but the *fjord-hest* seems the original and more ancient type.

The Norwegian-Fjord breeds true to type. It is thought to have origins similar to those of the Konik. Though Norway is its home, countries lacking their own native ponies have imported large numbers, particularly Denmark and Germany. Their strength and docile temperament has made them invaluable to farmers, and for transport.

108

A feature of the breed is a rather coarse mane, dark in the centre and light on the outside. It is usually clipped in a curve to give the neck more of a crest and to ensure that the dark internal line is slightly higher than the outside lighter hair. This is an ancient custom: drawings of ponies so clipped are found on Viking runestones.

Height 14 hands.

Colour A feature is the distinctiveness of its two colours – cream and dun. A dark dorsal stripe runs from tail to forelock through the mane. The legs are dark, and occasionally zebra markings occur. Bays and browns are also found, but dun is the prevailing and ancestral colour.

Conformation The Fjord pony has a well-shaped head with a broad and flat forehead and big eyes. The head is rather large but seldom common. The ears are small, truncated and rather broadly placed. The neck is short and thick, the connection between head and neck being somewhat stiff. The withers are rather short and round. The back is of medium length with well-developed muscles. The outer corner of the hip is far forward as compared with the inner corner and causes the croup to be narrow, but it also makes the pony more strongly coupled. The thighs are muscular but often rather shallow. The legs are dry and clean but a little coarse. The movement is light and quick.

Uses Fjord ponies are well suited for work on farms and in horticulture. They are used in all manner of harness work including competitions. They can be a good ride and are used as children's ponies and for vaulting by riders.

Oldenburg

The Oldenburg was the heaviest of the German warm-blood breeds. Originally it developed in northern Germany along the same lines as the East Friesian, but after World War II the area became part of the German Democratic Republic. Both breeds trace their ancestry to the Friesian of Holland, and through this to Spanish and Oriental stallions.

Named after Count Anton von Oldenburg, the Oldenburg has a long history, there being records of horses so named in the Thirty Years' War (1618–48). However, it was farmers who, during the last century, really established the breed as we know it today. They wanted big, strong horses to work in the fields and to go in harness, and they organized a breed society, importing foreign stallions such as Thoroughbred, Cleveland Bay, and Norman, also using the native Hanoverians from Lower Saxony. An important foundation stallion for one line was the Yorkshire Coach Horse 'Stavee'. From these strains they established a type which could work on their farms and be used by the army, particularly the artillery. Little outside blood was subsequently used until after World War II, when a lighter type of horse became needed. To achieve this, Anglo-Norman and Thoroughbred blood was infused (a successful addition being 'Lupus', a winner of the German Derby).

The original breeding grounds are the northwest of Germany. The breed is also very popular in Denmark, and some have been exported to improve or act as foundation stock for such breeds as the Lithuanian and Kladruber.

Height　16.2 to 17.2 hands.

Colour　Most solid colours.

Conformation　The head is a little plain, and straight in the face. The shoulder is strong, the body deep and muscular. The hindquarters are powerful and there is plenty of bone to the legs.

Uses　With good active movement, longevity and strength it has been used by farmers and riders for transport. Until recent additions of Thoroughbred blood it was best known for carriage work, and there are examples of it at the Royal Mews in London. Today the finer version is more of a riding horse and suitable for all competitions.

Orlov Trotter

The originator of this famous breed of Russian trotters was Count Alexius Grigorievich Orlov, a Russian nobleman who was born in 1737 and died in 1808. He was implicated in the conspiracy of 1762 which led to the death of Czar Peter III. He also commanded the Russian fleet which annihilated the Turks at Chesme in 1770. When he died he left 30,000 serfs and an estate worth five million rubles.

After his more violent activities he turned his attention to horse-breeding, and in 1777 evolved the breed which for ever after was to be known by his name. He produced the Orlov Horse by using

English Thoroughbred, Arab, Dutch, Danish, and Mecklenburg breeds. The first stallion was an Arab called 'Smetanka' which was put to a Dutch or Danish mare from whom was bred a stallion called 'Polkan'. The first trotter out of the latter's progeny was a stallion out of a black Dutch mare which was named 'Bars First'. This horse is considered to be the progenitor of the Orlov breed. There were further admixtures of Dutch, English and Arab blood.

The Orlov achieved its greatest fame in the latter half of the last century when it was looked upon as the supreme trotting horse, and more than 3,000 stud farms in Russia were devoted to its breeding. Many were destroyed at the time of the Revolution, but organized breeding was eventually re-established.

Today it cannot compete on equal terms with the strong commercial development of the trotting horse for the race track, mostly in America. The Orlov has thus been cross-bred to the American Standardbred (because the latter was considered to be faster), and the resultant offspring are known as Russian Trotters.

Height   It can grow to a height of 17 hands.

Colour   Grey and black.

Conformation   A good Orlov is a handsome, well-made horse. The small head still bears the Arab stamp. The chest is broad, the back longish, the hindquarters strong and well rounded, and the legs are muscular.

Uses   Trotting races, and as foundation stock for other breeds.

Palomino

Palomino is not yet strictly a breed, only a colour.
Its origins appear to be Spanish, from Arab and
Barb, Saracen and Moorish stock. Horses of this
colour became highly prized in Spain. Queen
Isabella, sponsor of Columbus, encouraged their
breeding and they were called 'Ysabellas' in her
honour. Such animals went with Cortes to Mexico
in 1519, and it is thought that they were named
after Juan de Palomino, to whom one was presented
by Cortes.

They were rediscovered nearly 140 years ago
when the United States took possession of California after the Mexican war. Thereafter they were

used extensively as saddlehorses, for parades and other spectacles, and also for racing until they were ousted by the speedier Thoroughbred.

The breeding is generally a cross between Palominos and light chestnuts of the light horse breeds, and also Palomino to Palomino. A cross between a chestnut mare with a light mane and tail and a Palomino stallion will in 80 per cent of such crosses produce a Palomino foal. The breeding is still in the experimental stage and is not fixed. The infusion of pony or draught blood is barred.

There are three main types of Palomino: the Parade (or Show) type; the Bridle Path type, a general utility saddlehorse; and the Stock Horse, for range work.

Foals are usually true Palomino at birth, with blue eyes, but with age the eyes darken and the colour changes. Manes and tails begin as chestnut, but whiten with age.

Height Varies.

Colour Golden, but there are five official shades with a metallic sheen, varying from a soft cream or light blonde chestnut to the darker shades. The mane and tail should be almost white, and except for white on the face and legs no other colours or markings are admitted; albino and pinto parentage are forbidden. The eyes are dark; blue or chalk eyes are not accepted.

Conformation Arab or Barb type, but larger and more solid. There are considerable variations.

Uses They are in demand as riding horses, particularly for classes in the show ring. They are also used for distance riding and for ranch work.

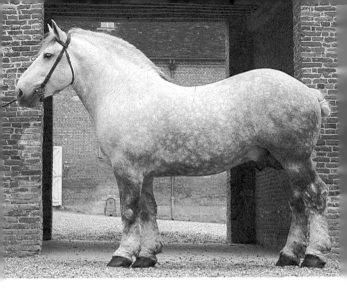

Percheron

The Percheron Horse is one of the most popular draught horses to be found at work today. Its popularity extends far beyond France where it originated, for it is renowned in Great Britain, several continental European countries, the USA, Canada and other parts of the world.

As in so many other cases, it is an admixture, based probably upon the working horses of Belgium and northern France, where a strong short-legged and active horse was the type required. Oriental infusions can be traced to the Middle Ages, the Arab most likely being responsible for the Percheron's unusual elegance and activity.

The credit for founding the Percheron horse is due to a small group of French farmers who about 130 years ago were farming an area not more than about 150 sq km (*c.* 60 sq m) in the district known as Le Perche, from which the horse takes its name. They produced an animal of outstanding qualities.

Height   Stallions not less than 16.3 hands and mares not less than 16.1 hands.

Colour   Grey or black only, with a minimum of white. Skin and coat of fine quality.

Conformation   The head is wide across the eyes, which are full and docile. The ears are of medium size, and erect. The expression is intelligent. The body is short, compact and strong. The neck is not short. The chest is wide, the shoulders deep and well laid; the back strong and short; the ribs wide and deep. The hindquarters are of exceptional width, and long from the hips to the tail. The limbs are short and strong with full second thighs, big knees and broad hocks. The bone is heavy and flat, the cannons short, the pasterns of medium length. The feet are of good quality, hard blue horn. The limbs are clean and usually free from hair. The action is straight and bold, with long, free strides rather than short, snappy ones. The hocks are well flexed and kept close.

Uses   This heavy horse is so active that in farming work it is a great saver of time. Yet it is docile and very easily handled. It is known for its good, hard, blue feet which enable it to stand up to work on the roads; it is thus useful for heavy transport. It has also provided important foundation stock for other breeds.

Peruvian Stepping Horse (Peruvian Paso)

This unusual breed stems from the Barb and Andalusian horses which were brought to Peru in the mid-sixteenth century and played a part in Pizarro's conquest of the country. The Barb is said to dominate the foundation stock, with the Andalusian contributing about one-quarter of the blood. It is likely that the Spanish Jennet also contributed.

The unique feature of this breed is the 'paso' gait. The horses are born with the ability to move their forelegs rather like paddles, in an extravagant action, while the hindlegs take long sweeping strides that usually overtrack the corresponding foreleg. The hindquarters are held low and the

118

back is held rigid. This is a very comfortable gait for the rider and is also very fast, with the horses being able to average 11 mph (18 km/h) and reach up to 15 mph (14 km/h). The gait is so balanced in this that they are able to maintain it even over very rough terrain, and for unusually long periods of time.

This lateral gait is similar to some of the gaits of the American breeds – such as the rack, the pace, the running walk and the singlefoot. It is said to have been derived from that of the medieval ambler.

The Paso's origin dates back over three centuries and in the ensuing years it has developed many of the attributes of the Criollo: tremendous toughness, powers of endurance, and ability to survive on poor keep.

The Paso Fino, which was developed in Puerto Rico, is said to be a close relation.

Height 14.2 to 15.2 hands.

Colour Most colours, but usually bay or chestnut.

Conformation General appearance is of Arab or Barb type, but larger and more solid. There are considerable variations, colour being the major criterion for entry into the stud book. They have very long hindlegs, long pasterns and great flexibility of the joints.

Uses With their kind disposition and showy action they are in demand as riding horses, particularly for classes in the show ring. They have great powers of endurance and are used for distance riding as well as for ranch work.

Pinto

The Pinto, or Paint Horse, covers all those strangely marked black-and-white and bay- or brown-and-white horses also known respectively as piebald and skewbald.

Examples of this peculiar colouring, which is a result of the combined action of albinism (whiteness), melanism (blackness) and erythema (redness) on the skin, are found all over the world and in most breeds of horses, but more especially in the primitive types.

The Pinto is not strictly a breed. Horses of this coloration, however, are widely prevalent all over North and South America, and the modern Pinto is recognized a a distinctive American horse. They have had a reputation for toughness and endurance, and with the added advantage of their natural camouflage were always favourites with the American Indian as war and ceremonial horses. They are now equally popular with American riders, and ranches in Canada and the USA are devoted to breeding them.

The Pinto strain is very potent and will reproduce itself fairly constantly. Special classes for these horses have been introduced into American shows, and the accepted judging rule is 50% for markings and 50% for conformation and performance.

Height Varies.

Colour There are two types of patterns. In Overo markings the white patches always originate from the belly and extend upwards. The back, mane and tail are generally dark. Dark and white alternate on the legs, which are rarely all white. White faces and glass (blue) eyes are usual.

The Tobiano pattern has no regular place of origin, white patches starting often from the back. Also the white and coloured areas are usually larger and nearly always solid. White legs are more often found, but the white face and glass eye are rarer. The dark patches in both cases are mostly black, brown and bay. Tobiano horses tend to be larger and heavier than Overos.

Conformation This varies, except that most specimens have thick necks and rather heavy shoulders.

Uses They are popular for general riding and in the show-ring, and are used as cow ponies.

121

Quarter Horse

The American Quarter Horse originated in Virginia and the Carolinas in the very early days of settlement. Because of the lack of cleared sites for courses, the first horse races in North America were run along 'race paths', which were cut out of the virgin wilderness and were usually about a quarter of a mile (0.4 km) long. The horse bred to race on these tracks was for this reason called the 'Quarter Horse'.

Obviously a very quick starter and fast sprinter was required, and in due course a specific type was produced, originally from a cross of Thoroughbred stallions and native mares. The latter were thought to be of Oriental background (Arabs and Barbs) as well as Andalusians, probably brought to Florida by the Spanish in the seventeenth century.

From a genealogical point of view the Quarter Horse breed starts from an English Thoroughbred, 'Janus', which was at stud in Virginia and North Carolina between 1756 and 1780. His racing distance when in England was 4 miles (6.4 km) but his progeny were noted for speed over short distances and had few equals in quarter-racing. 'Janus' stood 14.2 hands and had particularly powerful hindquarters, with great prominent muscles.

Height 14.3 to 16.1 hands.

Colour Any solid colour, usually chestnut. White markings are not allowed on the belly and such horses cannot be registered.

Conformation They are a compact powerful shape, standing close to the ground. They have heavy frames which are extremely well muscled up, especially in the hindquarters, loin and back. The withers are low.

Uses Their most valuable function is still as racehorses. Quarter Horse racing is big business in the USA, their speed over distances of 180 to 365 m (200 to 400 yd) being spectacular. Their athleticism and calm temperament ensure their popularity with cattlemen. Their fast starting and sprinting enable them to head off any beasts, while their strength and nimbleness provide them with the power to catch up with and hold a heavy steer when it is roped. These talents are also of value in their other major activity as rodeo horses. They are used, too, for general riding and showing.

Saddlebred

This American breed dates back to the early
settlements, when good horses were essential for
covering the vast distances of the new continent.
As there were no indigenous horses, the pioneers
brought their own or imported them soon after
arrival: principally English amblers and pacers
(this was before the time of the Thoroughbred)
together with horses from Spain, France, Africa
and the East. All these were used in the development of the American Saddlebred.

The pioneers needed a speedy animal, comfortable to ride over long distances and adaptable to
harness. Accordingly they bred selectively from

the best stock available. The English Thoroughbred later gave the breed its fire and brilliance, and
various American stocks, such as the Morgan and
Standardbred were introduced. Though the official
founder of today's Saddlebred is 'Denmark', foaled
in 1839, the parent of the breed was the earlier-
established Kentucky Saddle Horse.

The speciality of the breed is its gaits, exhibited
nowadays in the show ring. These are the walk,
trot and canter, also the slow gait and the rack. The
horses are known as Three- or Five-gaited according to the number of gaits for which they have
been trained. In the rack each foot comes down
singly and with great speed, sounding a steady 1-
2-3-4- with each beat equal. The slow gait is as seen
in a good trotting camel, the feet on each side
following each other instead of stepping diagonally
as in the normal trot.

These horses performing their gaits are a
memorable spectacle, and even in the normal trot
the action is unusually high, smooth and speedy.

Height   15 to 16 hands.

Colour   Black, brown, bay, grey, chestnut.

Conformation   The Saddlebred is light and elegant, with a good head, long, fine neck, well-sloped
shoulders, round barrel, flat croup and good clean
legs. The mane and tail are very full. The general
appearance is of 'breeding' and brilliance, with
high proud carriage of head and tail and a stance
that covers plenty of ground.

Uses   Most Saddlebreds are directed at the show-
ring where they are shown off under saddle or in
harness. Some are used for general riding.

Schleswig

This horse is bred in the western part of Schleswig
Province in northwest Germany. In the Middle
Ages it was appreciated and used for much the
same purposes as the Friesian – as a strong active
saddle horse to carry the heavily armoured knights.
Since that time its breeding has been well patron-
ized by German rulers.

Establishment of the breed as we know it today
began at the end of the nineteenth century when
the Schleswig Breeders' Association was organized
to control breeding and to produce a type which
could be useful as both an artillery horse and a
heavy cart-horse. A stud book was started in 1891.

Schleswig Province belonged at one time to Denmark, and the breeding of the Schleswig and Jutland horses are similar. 'Oppenheim LXII', the Suffolk/Shire stallion from Britain, who had such an influence on the Jutland, also played a major part in the development of the Schleswig. The interchange of blood between the Jutland and the Schleswig continued into the twentieth century, but since 1938 no Danish stallions have been used. The horse sometimes had faults such as a tendency to soft feet and a rather too long back. To counteract these, further cross-breeding was decided upon, and other breeds which have figured in the development of the Schleswig include Breton, Boulonnais, Thoroughbred and Yorkshire Coach Horse. The result of the use of the Thoroughbred and other warm-bloods is that it has been considerably lightened and made more active. Many consider that it should no longer be called a cold-blood, for it has become a cob-like horse, although still heavy.

Height   15.1 to 16 hands.

Colour   Chestnut with flaxen mane and tail.

Conformation   The head is rather large and a little common with a convex face. The neck is short and thick, but well arched. The body is very strong and broad, with indistinctive withers. The legs are short and have very little feather on them.

Uses   These relatively active and good moving horses are tractable and easy to work. They have always been very popular with farmers and can be used for all types of draught work.

Selle Français

Since 1958 all French riding horses other than
Arabs, Thoroughbreds and Anglo-Arabs have
been categorized as Selle Français if they have
pedigrees (they are Cheval de Selle if origins are
unknown). The most famous breed to accede to it
is the Anglo-Norman, developed from the medieval Norman war horse and refined in the late
eighteenth and early nineteenth centuries through
crossing with Arab, Thoroughbred, and Norfolk
Trotter. In Normandy the soil, rich in lime and
iron, and the temperate weather, are very condu-
cive to the breeding of strong horses.

It was from the Anglo-Norman that the French

Trotter developed; but the ancestor of today's riding horse was the type used by the cavalry.

The Limousin is another fine breed of riding horse now known as Selle Français; an Arab type, its origins date back to the eighth-century Moorish invasion. Improved by alternate crossing with English Thoroughbred and Arab and, later, with Anglo-Normans to give it size and substance, it still retains its Thoroughbred and Arab features.

The Vendéen or Charentais was another foundation breed for the Selle Français. It dates back to the seventeenth century when the mares of Charente and Vendée were crossed with imports from Holland. Subsequent cross-breeding with Norman and Anglo-Norman and with Thoroughbred, Arab, Anglo-Arab and Norfolk blood have further upgraded it.

So superior was the Anglo-Norman half-bred – in terms of substance, sensible temperament and athleticism – that it was continually used for cross-breeding. Thus the various regional French riding horse breeds were progressively amalgamated.

The variety of breeds involved in the Selle Français is shown by the following figures: 33 per cent of Selle Français have a Thoroughbred sire, 20 per cent Anglo-Arab, 45 per cent Selle Français, and 2 per cent Trotter. With this variety of backgrounds the height, colour, and conformation differ considerably.

Uses Selle Français, an athletic, energetic horse with substance, is a top competition horse. Particularly successful as a show jumper and event horse, it is also suitable for general riding.

Shagya

The Shagya is a special kind of Arab half-bred developed in Hungary from native stock and from a stallion of that name. 'Shagya' was born in Syria in 1830 and bought by the Hungarians from the Bedouin to stand at the Babolna Stud near Bana. Following tradition, stallions of this breed all have the same name, with the addition of a Roman number which shows to which generation the horse belongs. Genetically the breed has been very well established, thanks to much careful in-breeding.

The native Hungarian stock has an interesting history. Equine skulls dating from the period of the Magyar invasion (c. tenth century AD) show that the Hungarian horse had prevailing characteristics of the wild Tarpan with a certain admixture of the blood of the Mongolian horse. It was a hard, primitive breed – late-maturing, small, and with great powers of endurance.

Following numerous Turkish invasions, the Hungarian horse was infused with a strong dose of Oriental blood by crossing with Arab, Turkish and Persian stallions. The Hungarian farm horse stems from these origins, and it was from this type of native stock that Hungarian horses – bred on a large scale for military purposes in the days of the Austro-Hungarian Empire – were largely developed.

The principal centre for the development of the Shagya was Babolna, but strains were also developed at Radovec, and at the Topolcianky and Kladruby-on-Elbe studs in Czechoslovakia. As its reputation grew, so the Shagya was exported further and further afield. After 1918 many of the stallions were sent to Poland where they appeared to improve the Polish breeding, especially in the southern part of the country. The breed was even exported as far away as the USA.

Height 14 to 15 hands.

Colour Usually grey.

Conformation Similar to the Arab.

Uses Its extreme hardiness, excellent movement, and ability to thrive on very little food made it into one of the best light cavalry and light carriage horses. Today it is also used for competitions.

Shetland

The Shetland is one of the world's smallest breeds of pony, yet is probably the strongest member of the equine race in relation to its size.

Its origin is uncertain, but there is evidence of its existence in the Shetland Isles as early as about 500 BC. Its diminutive size has been attributed to the severe climate there; but generations bred in warmer areas seem to remain equally small.

There was no attempt at selective breeding until the middle of the nineteenth century, when the pony was first used in the coal pits. Previously its use in the Islands was as a saddle pony and as a pack pony, often for carting seaweed for use as

132

manure. Demand from the coal mines stimulated the breeding of Shetlands, but as the buyers took the best, the stock became very poor in quality, until the 5th Marquess of Londonderry established a stud in 1870 in the islands of Bressay and Noss. His stallion 'Jack', became famous as a foundation sire and has had a profound influence on the breed.

Height Registered stock must not exceed 40 in at three years old and 42 in at four years and over.

Colour Black is the foundation colour, but Shetlands can be bay, brown, chestnut, grey and particolour. The pony has a double coat in winter and a smooth one in summer.

Conformation Head well-shaped. Broad forehead, with fairly straight foreface and pleasing eye. Neck rises off a well-laid oblique shoulder, with a good crest. Body is thickset and deep ribbed, with short back, broad chest and quarters, profuse mane and tail, and feathering of straight hair. Loins strong and muscular. Forelegs well placed under the shoulder and chest, and standing plumb with well-muscled forearm, strong knees followed through by a good flat bone. Hind thighs strong and muscular with broad hocks followed through by good flat bone and pasterns. Feet round.

Uses Today the major market is as a child's saddle pony. It is also used increasingly for harness work, and in speed competitions is very fast between obstacles.

It has a quaint beauty quite unlike that of any other breed, and with its lovable character it is deservedly popular, often kept just as a pet.

Shire

Both in height and weight the Shire Horse is the largest of England's agricultural horses. At one time it was widely used as a draught horse in all large towns throughout the country, but the breed really belongs to the Midlands and Fens of East Anglia.

The Shire traces its ancestry back to the Old Black English Cart-horse of the eighteenth century, and further back still to the importations of black horses probably of Flemish origin.

It has often been said that the armoured knights of the Middle Ages were mounted on these extremely heavy animals, but it is far more likely that they rode stout, strong cobs.

In England the Shire is now bred largely in the deep and heavy-soiled counties of Lincoln and Cambridge, where its enormous strength makes it popular as an agricultural horse. It is capable of pulling a net weight of 5.08 tonnes (5 tons) and although perhaps the slowest worker of the heavy breeds it is a steady, level mover of great honesty.

Height The best of the breed stand over 17 hands.

Colour Bays and browns are the predominant colours, while blacks and greys are less frequent, and all Shires have a considerable amount of white on the feet and legs.

Conformation Head lean in proportion to body, neither too large nor too small. Forehead broad between the eyes. Eyes large, prominent and docile in appearance. Nostrils thin and wide, lips together and nose slightly Roman. Ears long, lean, sharp and sensitive. Throat clean-cut and lean. Shoulders deep, oblique and wide enough for the collar to rest on. Neck fairly long, slightly arched, and well set up, to give the horse a commanding appearance. Limbs strong with great bone and heavy feather.

Uses In character this great horse is of a docile nature, and it can be worked at three years old. Though the demand for farm horses has diminished there has been a great revival in their breeding in England. They are such handsome imposing animals that they are popular in the show ring, and many are exported.

Standardbred

This is the famous trotting and pacing horse of the USA, where harness racing, whether trotting or pacing (which is the lateral movement as opposed to the diagonal), is very popular.

The father of the modern Standardbred was William M. Rysdyk's 'Hambletonian', also known as 'Hambletonian 10' from his Standard number in the Register. Foaled in 1849, he was descended in three ways (direct male line and two collateral crosses) from the English Thoroughbred 'Messenger', the *fons et origo* of all American trotting horses, who himself was the son of the Thoroughbred 'Mambrino'. Through him the breed goes back in the male line via 'Blaze' to the Darley Arabian. The pedigree of almost every Standardbred can be traced back to one of Hambletonian's four sons. Allied with this principal foundation element are many other Thoroughbred strains, also Morgan, Norfolk Trotter and other light horse strains. The Norfolk Trotter 'Bellfounder', imported into America in 1788, was a special influence.

The Standardbred as a breed dates officially from 1879, when the National Association of Trotting Horse Breeders adopted a set of rules governing admission to the American Trotting Register (first published in 1871). The rules have been varied from time to time according to the progress made in the establishment of the type. Today the 'Standard', having been originally based largely on performance and speed on the race track, now relates to blood only. Selective breeding has transformed an initially composite type into a homogenous and firmly established one. Trotting horses world-wide owe something to the American breed, as most countries have imported them to upgrade their own stock.

Height   14 to 16 hands.

Colour   Most solid colours.

Conformation   The Standardbred is a Thoroughbred type, with modification due to differences in gait and work. It tends to be heavier limbed and more robustly built, with longer body, shorter legs and greater endurance.

Uses   Its heart, stamina and speed make it a leading trotter or pacer. It is also used to upgrade the stock of other countries.

Suffolk

The Suffolk Horse, which is also known as the
Suffolk Punch, is always chestnut in colour. It is
also the only clean-legged British draught horse. It
is indigenous to the County of Suffolk and,
according to Camden's *Britannia*, dates back to
1506. A feature of the breed is that every specimen
now in existence traces its descent in direct male
line in an unbroken chain to a trotting horse called
'Blakes Farmer' foaled in 1760.

Although for a long time one of the purest
breeds, it has been influenced by some infusion
from Norfolk Trotters and Cobs and even a little
Thoroughbred, producing a very handsome horse

with a fine record of performance.

The Suffolk will work well as a two-year-old and go on until it is in its mid-twenties. It is also very economical to keep, doing well on little and poor feed. With rare exceptions, it is very docile. Old records in the form of advertisements show that pulling contests were held in the County of Suffolk, which would seem to prove that its great strength has long been recognized.

Height About 16 hands.

Colour Chestnut. A star or a little white on the face is accepted.

Conformation Unlike the Clydesdale, it should have great width in front and in the hindquarters. Another feature is its short legs and consequent low draught, giving it a great direct pull on its vehicle. It can trot smart and true, with well-balanced and good action.

The head is big, with a broad forehead. Neck deep in the collar, tapering gracefully towards the setting of the head. Shoulders long and muscular, well thrown back at wither. Body deep and round-ribbed from shoulder to flank. The legs should be straight with fair sloping pasterns, big knees and long clean hocks on short cannon-bones free from coarse hair. Elbows turned in are regarded as a serious defect. Feet have plenty of size with circular form protecting the frog.

Uses Some cross-breeding with Thoroughbreds and Arabs to produce heavyweight riding horses, but the produce is not consistent. The Suffolk is still used for draught work in East Anglia and is popular in the show-ring.

Swedish Warm-Blood

The Swedish Warm-blood is one of the most successful competition horses, having won gold medals at the Olympics in all disciplines.

The breed was evolved to mount the Swedish cavalry on homebred rather than imported stock. Native stock (which tended to be of pony origin) was put to carefully selected imports, which were mainly Hanoverian, Trakehner and Thoroughbred. This policy was introduced at the end of the nineteenth century, and by the 1930s the number of Swedish warm-bloods showing the qualities required had become sufficient to minimize the need for further imports. The stud book however, has never been closed to carefully selected outside breeds. If the Swedish Warm-Blood shows a tendency to lack a required feature, then stallions are imported which have been carefully chosen to inject this particular asset.

Cross-breeding is highly selective, and one of the features of the breed's development has been the rigorous standards laid down for stock. Entry into the stud book, which was first started in 1874, is allowed only after thorough veterinary examination, and inspections for conformation, temperament and action. Additionally, the stallions are put through dressage, show jumping, cross-country and pulling tests. If they pass, they may be bred from. But only after their progeny has been examined (after they have been three years at stud) are they given a full breeding licence.

Some privately owned stallions are found at stud, but the most highly prized are those that are state-owned and which stand at the stud at Flyinge in the south of Sweden.

Height 15 to 17 hands.

Colour Any solid colour.

Conformation Intelligent head, with bold, large eyes. The neck tends to be long and crested. The body is tough and wiry. The feet can be rather long and narrow.

Uses These athletic, intelligent horses are top class performers in eventing and dressage; they are also driven, and used for general riding. They have been used to upgrade other nations' warm-bloods.

Tarpan

This ancient strain of wild horse has contributed to the ancestry of most European and some Eastern breeds of horses and ponies. The forest Tarpan (*Equus przevalskii gmelini* Antonius) once roamed the forests of central and eastern Europe, whilst the steppe Tarpan was found in herds south of the Ural mountains. There is some confusion between the two ancient strains of horse, with Przevalski's Horse (Mongolian/Asian Wild Horse) sometimes even being referred to as a Tarpan.

Tarpans were hunted extensively, and by the late eighteenth century were close to extinction except for a few kept in reserves, such as that of

Count Zamoyski in Poland. During the nineteenth century even these were caught and domesticated by the peasants, but some small and primitive ponies, with many characteristics of their ancestors, the wild Tarpans, survived in the forests and backward areas around Zamoyski's reserve until the end of World War II.

Professor T. Vetulani, an authority on primitive horses, decided in the 1930s to use the Zamoyski animals to regenerate the Forest Tarpan. In 1936 they were collected and taken to a special reserve in Bialowiecz forest in Poland (now a National Park), where they were kept in wild conditions and fed hay only in winter. In 1939 there were three stallions, 13 mares and 19 foals but a number died during World War II. In 1955 all the animals were transferred to the reserve at Popiellno. There the two herds now live natural lives without shelter or veterinary attention, whilst a domesticated herd is kept at the Science Centre for special study.

Many generations have now survived and numbers have increased. The Forest Tarpan thus once more lives the life of a wild horse.

Height   Around 13 hands.

Colour   The coat is generally mouse-dun or blue-dun, with some striping on the legs, and sometimes striping on the entire body. Black mane and tail and a black dorsal stripe are common to all animals. In winter some grow a longer, whiter coat.

Conformation   The head is rather big, long and broad. The ears are also long, as is the back.

Uses   As subjects of research in their two reserves. Used for light agricultural work.

Tennessee Walking Horse

The Tennessee Walking Horse is also known in
the USA as the Plantation Walking Horse, which
indicates the special purpose for which it was
produced – to carry farmers and planters of the
South at a comfortable pace around their planta-
tions. It was also sometimes known as the Turn-
Row, because it could be ridden between rows of
crops without causing damage.

Like the Morgan Horse, this breed owes its
foundation to one powerful prepotent stallion, who
was known as 'Black Allan' because of his colour.
He was a Standardbred trotting stallion of mixed
Hambletonian and Morgan ancestry. Foaled in

1886, he was taken to Tennessee as a colt, and like 'Justin Morgan', the progenitor of the Morgan, had a long life at stud and produced numerous progeny, mainly from the Tennessee mares of mixed Thoroughbred, pacing and saddle horse strains. He was a sire of great prepotency, reproducing his type regularly.

The breed was a natural production of the needs of place and time, and later established itself as a popular and useful type on its own merits.

Its unique feature is a special gait called the 'running walk', which is fast, comfortable and enduring. This made the Tennessee Walking Horse a speedy, pleasing means of transport and as such it was much favoured by Southern planters and farmers. Careful training, however, is needed to develop the true running gait, which is liable to turn into the 'pace'.

Height 15 to 16 hands.

Colour Most common are bays, blacks and chestnuts, but roans and greys are found.

Conformation The Walking Horse is a much heavier and more powerful animal than the American Saddlebred, and is generally larger, stouter, more robust and less elegant than the latter. The head is large and plain, the neck rather short, the body and hindquarters solid and massive, and the limbs have good bone.

Uses It is equable of disposition, intelligent and well-mannered. This makes it a first-class general-purpose animal, useful on the farm, between the shafts or under the saddle. Today, with its unique gait, it is popular as a show horse.

Tersky

These horses are bred and were developed in the Stavropol region (North Caucasus) of the Soviet Union. The breed is a young one, started only in the 1920s and officially established in 1948. An Arab-type horse was wanted, and the main foundation stock was the now extinct breed of Strelets (a large Arab based on native Ukrainian mares and selected Oriental sires), Arabs, Kabardin and Don horses. The breeding centre was the state stud of Tersk, from which the horse is named.

With this foundation stock a horse was established which had the characteristics of the Oriental breeds (elegance and movement) combined with the toughness of the native breeds.

There are three types of Tersky: the character-istic type; the light Eastern type; and the thickset version. The characteristic type is described below. The light Eastern type is similar except that it is closer to the Arab, and with a finer head, a more concave face, and shorter finer legs. It is also a little more delicate and elegant. The thickset type, on the other hand, has more bone, is slightly taller, and tends to be longer in the body.

Height   14.3 to 15.1 hands.

Colour   Grey which often has a silver sheen. Chestnuts and bays are also found.

Conformation   The head is medium sized, and the profile tends to be straight (except in the Eastern version), with large eyes. The ears are long, as are the neck and the back. The hindquarters are wide and muscular, the tail is set-on high like that of the Arab. The bone is fine and flat, the hooves strong.

Uses   Tersky horses are intelligent, good-natured, agile, good movers and capable of considerable endurance. They are used for racing, but against Arabs not against Thoroughbreds. They are particularly adept at endurance work and endur-ance races and are used by the army both under saddle and in harness. They are popular for competition, and general riding, and are in demand for circus work. Today they are also being used to improve other breeds.

Thoroughbred

The Thoroughbred is synonymous with today's racehorse, and is the best known of all British Breeds.

All Thoroughbreds trace their ancestry to three famous Eastern sires, imported to England in the late seventeenth and early eighteenth centuries – the Byerley Turk, the Darley Arabian, and the Godolphin Barb. Although it has often been claimed that they were put to English mares, there is evidence that some of the foundation mares were Eastern.

During the eighteenth century less and less Arab blood was introduced, the desire for more

148

speed and for early maturity becoming paramount. Today's Arab cannot match the Thoroughbred for speed, but has greater endurance.

The Thoroughbred's value is based almost entirely on its speed and those unsuccessful in races are of little value at stud. The slower horses can be used as steeplechasers, hunters, or competition horses, or to produce these.

Height   Varies; average about 16 hands.

Colour   Most whole colours.

Conformation   Head refined, neck elegant and arched, withers pronounced, shoulder sloping. Legs hard, clean, of good bone, with tendons pronounced. Back not too long, body deep, ribs well-sprung to barrel shape. The tail should be well set; hindquarters generous, with hocks well let down, standing true and moving with great sweeping action indicative of great speed.

Uses   The Thoroughbred's main use is in flat-racing, a sport that has become a national industry in many countries (eg, USA, Australia, France, England, Ireland and Japan). It is also much used for steeplechasing in France and the British Isles, and to some extent in the USA. No other breed can ever supplant it in racing, because of its speed.

Along with the Arab, the Thoroughbred is the main source of upgrading in order to inject speed and class into breeds such as the Hanoverian and for cross-breeding with horses of substance – particularly in the British Isles – to produce types such as hunters, hacks, and polo ponies. The British Thoroughbred has been exported as foundation stock for every other country's racing stock.

American Thoroughbred 'Wajima'

The French Thoroughbred became an official national breed during the 1830s, and was based on English Thoroughbreds imported since the late eighteenth century. The French horses are particularly renowned for staying power. 'Monarque', the first truly great French Thoroughbred, founded a most successful line. Other influential sires were the grey 'Le Sancy', 'Dollar', 'St Simon', 'Galopin', and 'Brantôme'.

At first, races were restricted to horses bred and raised in France, but in 1863 the Grand Prix de Paris, an international race, was founded. Two years later, when 'Gladiateur' won the British

150

Triple Crown, French Thoroughbreds began to gain substantial recognition outside France.

The revival of French Thoroughbred racing after World War II was largely due to Marcel Boussac, at whose Fresnay-le-Buffard Stud 'Tourbillon' and 'Pharos' produced many outstanding racehorses. Baron Guy de Rothschild at Méautry, Madame Volterra, Jean Stern, François Dupré and Prince Aly Khan also made important contributions.

Thoroughbred breeding is mainly concentrated in Normandy and around Paris. While most are bred for racing, Thoroughbreds are also used on mares of various breeds in an aim to upgrade them.

Italian Thoroughbred. Italy's heyday in racehorse breeding was before and after World War I. Outstanding produce included 'Nearco' (sire of 'Dante'), 'Donatello II' and 'Ribot'. All were bred by Frederico Tesio, perhaps the most successful and influential racehorse breeder in the world.

North American Thoroughbred. The USA was the first overseas territory to introduce racing British style. They have imported and bred Thoroughbreds since the end of the seventeenth century.

The American racing and breeding industry is now the largest and most commercial in the world; since World War II its horses have become consistent international winners. This success is due in part to the importing of such great stallions as 'Mahmound', 'Blenheim', 'Nasrullah' and 'Ribot', and in part to the tremendous interest and huge sums invested in the sport and in breeding for it.

Toric

In Estonia in the northern USSR the most popular
farm horse has been the Toric. A strong but small
cold-blood capable of most types of work on the
farm, it was developed at the Toric stud from the
local Kleppers which were strong, cobby types
produced by crossing the ponies of the Baltic States
with Arab and Ardennes stallions. They were the
working ponies of Estonia but since their name
only meant 'nag', they were never really established
as a breed. These dun ponies, however, were
prepotent for toughness and hardiness and they
did contribute towards the establishment of breeds
other than the Toric, such as the Viatka.

During the nineteenth century efforts were made to upgrade the Klepper, and these led to the development of the Toric. A good deal of outside blood was used; it included Orlov Trotter, Arab, Ardennes, and Thoroughbred. At the beginning of the twentieth century, further imports were bought and there was cross-breeding with Hanoverian, East Friesian and East Prussian stallions. As systematic selection was used in this cross-breeding, the result was a high class working horse with particularly good paces, and even with the athletic ability to jump well.

Two types have developed – the light and the heavy – the former being used for riding and the latter for harness work. In conformation they are fairly similar, differing mainly in size of bone and weight-carrying capacity.

Colour   Chestnut is most common but bays are found.

Height   15 to 15.1 hands.

Conformation   The head is of a medium size, with a wide forehead, erect ears and large eyes and nostrils. The neck is strong, the withers broad but not high. The back is straight, the hindquarters powerful. The legs are short and there is light feather on them.

Uses   Their calm temperament, adaptable nature and good movement makes them popular both for riding and harness work. They were originally bred mainly for farm work.

Trakehner

The Trakehner, sometimes known as the East
Prussian, was bred in that area, the largest horse
breeding centre of the German army before the
end of World War II.

Before the war the breeding of East Prussian
foals and their sale as yearlings was an extremely
profitable business. The 10,000 members of the
breeding association had 20,000 mares registered,
while four State studs bred army remounts from
500 stallions and 33,000 mares.

Most influential in the foundation of the breed
was the Trakehnen Stud, founded in 1732 by
Frederick William I of Prussia. The foundation

breeding material came from Royal Studs and high class Arabs. Local Schweiken stock was used, then Thoroughbreds were imported, and Trakehners soon became the most prized cavalry horses.

The Trakehnen Stud was destroyed during World War II, but today the breed thrives both in the southern area of East Prussia (now part of Poland) and in West Germany, where some of the original stock was taken in 1944 by a group fleeing from the Russians.

The Trakehner has been fostered with characteristic German thoroughness. At the Trakehnen Stud three-year-olds were rigorously trained and as four-year-olds were put through trials which included hunting with a pack of hounds and cross-country races. The very best horses were retained for breeding in the Trakehnen Stud; the next best went to State studs and a third class to private breeders. These three successful classes were branded with double elk antlers. The unsuccessful were castrated and used as army remounts.

Today the breeding stock in West Germany is put through similar tests at Neumünster.

Height Around 16.1 hands but varies.

Colour Any solid colour, usually dark.

Conformation The head, particularly broad between the eyes, narrows towards the muzzle. The neck long and crested, the shoulder sloping. Withers are prominent; hindquarters a little straight.

Uses Their extravagant action, elegant conformation and good temperament make them excellent competition and general riding horses.

Viatka

The Viatka is one of the primitive type breeds of pony produced in the Baltic states of the USSR. They have bred relatively free from the influence of man, and although there has been a little cross-breeding they closely resemble their remote ancestors. Today the purity of the breed is more secure because Viatkas are produced on state studs where cross-breeding is prevented.

There are a number of these primitive type pony breeds in the Baltic states, all quite similar in appearance and closely related to the Konik (qv) and the Klepper (see Toric). These include the Pechora and Zemaituka, but the best known is the

Viatka. Its home is in the Udmurt Republic and Kirov district, and it was originally bred in the Viatsky territory which lies along the Viatka river. As its popularity grew its breeding spread into the neighbouring regions and two types developed – the Obwinski and the Kasanski – which were named after the regions where they were found.

The Viatka is a little larger than its ancestor the Konik, but it possesses the Konik's useful primitive characteristics of strength, frugality and stamina. It also displays the dorsal stripe common to the primitive ponies of eastern Europe.

The Viatka's ability to survive extremely cold weather is largely due to possession of an unusually thick coat and subcutaneous layer of fat.

Height   13 to 15 hands.

Colour   Palomino, dun or chestnut with a dark dorsal stripe.

Conformation   Plain longish head with a particularly wide forehead and a slightly concave profile. The lower jaw can be massive. The neck is long, the wither relatively high. The chest is deep and strong, the shoulders sloping. The back is broad, straight and long. The legs are short with good bone. The forelegs tend to be rather wide apart, and the hocks are often 'sickle'.

Uses   These short quick striding ponies with their spirited temperaments are all rounders, used in harness and under saddle. They are popular for lighter farm work and for general transport. They are the ponies used most frequently to pull the troikas – the sleighs harnessed to three horses abreast.

Welsh Cob and Welsh Pony (Cob Type)

The Welsh Cob, an animal of many virtues and outstanding strength and activity, derives from the Welsh Mountain Pony. Andalusian blood was said to have been introduced in the twelfth century.

It has had great influence on trotting animals in many countries, and its blood contributed towards the Fell Pony and the British Hackney Horse and Pony.

The Welsh cob is very active and, in pre-mechanized days, was much used for military packwork and for mounted infantry, being capable of bearing an enormous weight. Its principal work in the past however, was for Welsh farmers, who used it to hunt, work on the farms, pull the family in a carriage, and even to race as a trotter.

The Cob is covered by Section D of the Welsh Pony and Cob Society's Stud Book. Apart from its height its features are similar to those of the Welsh Pony (Cob type), covered by Section C of the book.

Height　Welsh Cob 14 to 15.1 hands.

Welsh Pony (Cob type) not over 13.2 hands.

Colour　Any except piebald or skewbald.

Conformation　Strong, hardy, with considerable substance. Quality head. Eyes bold, prominent, wide apart. Ears neat, well set. Neck lengthy, well carried. Shoulders strong, well laid back. Forelegs set square; long, strong forearms. Well developed knees with plenty of bone below. Pasterns of proportionate slope and length, feet well shaped, hooves dense. Some silky feather. Back and loins strong, well coupled; deep through heart, well ribbed up. Hindquarters lengthy, strong; tail well set on. Second thighs strong; hocks large, flat, clean, and not set behind line from hindquarter point to fetlock joint; points prominent and not turning in or out. Pasterns and feet as on forelegs. Action with the knee bending and the whole foreleg extending straight from shoulder and as far forward as possible in the trot. Hocks flex under body with straight and powerful leverage.

Uses　These active utility types, still used by Welsh farmers for work and pleasure, are becoming increasingly popular for harness work, particularly in showing and combined driving. Show classes for the breed in-hand are numerous. The Cob is used, too, for breeding competition horses.

Welsh Mountain and Welsh Pony

Many consider the Welsh Mountain Pony the most beautiful of Britain's native ponies. It is indigenous to the Welsh mountains and wastes, where it still thrives wild or semi-wild. Its ancestry and upbringing give it intelligence, pluck, soundness and endurance. Though so small in height, it carries full grown men without apparent effort. It was much used as a pit pony.

It is claimed that Welsh Pony mares played a part in the very early breeding of the English Thoroughbred. It was certainly much used for producing the Polo Pony, the Hackney, the Hack and the Hunter as well as the Welsh Cob.

Height Ponies not exceeding 12 hands form Section A of the Stud Book.

Colour Any except piebald and skewbald.

Conformation Head small, clean-cut, well set-on and tapering to the muzzle. Eyes bold. Ears small, pointed. Nostrils prominent and open. Jaws and throat clean and finely cut, with ample room at the jaw angle. Neck lengthy, well carried. Shoulders long, well-sloped back. Withers moderately fine. The humerus upright, the foreleg not set-in under the body. Forelegs square and true, not tied in at elbow. Long strong forearms; well developed knee, short flat bone below knee; pasterns of proportionate slope and length; feet well-shaped, round. Hooves dense. Back and loins muscular, strong, well coupled. Girth deep. Ribs well sprung. Hindquarters lengthy and fine. Tail well set-on, carried gaily. Hindlegs: hocks large, flat and clean with points prominent, to turn neither in nor out; hindleg not too bent; the hock not behind a line from the point of the hindquarter to the fetlock joint; pasterns of proportionate length and slope; feet well shaped; hooves dense. Action quick free and straight from the shoulder, well away in the front; hocks well flexed, with straight powerful leverage, well under the body.

Uses For the show-ring and as children's ponies.

The larger version, known as the Welsh Pony, forms Section B of the stud book. It does not exceed 13.2 hands and is similar to the Welsh Mountain, except that it should be more of a riding-pony, with bone and substance, hardiness and constitution.

Westphalian

The Westphalian, like most warm-bloods bred for riding and competition, has no closed stud book and therefore is not pure-bred. Stallions standing at the State Stud of Warendorf include Thoroughbreds and Hanoverians as well as Westphalians. If born in the area and out of a registered mare, the horses are Westphalians and may be branded as such. During the 1970s they came to be recognized as among the best competition horses in the world. Their first major success was when 'Roman' won the World Show Jumping Championship in 1978. At the World Championships of 1982 they completed a double, winning the show jumping ('Fire')

162

and dressage ('Ahlerich') titles.

The breed has quite a long history, the breeders' association having been formed in 1826. During this century the stock has been based on its successful neighbour, the Hanoverian, of which the Westphalian looks like a heavier and thicker-set version.

The West German Ministry of Agriculture owns the State Stud of Warendorf, where stallions can only stand after they have been through pedigree, anatomy, character and riding tests. Potential Westphalian stallions are tested for tractive power as $3\frac{1}{2}$-year-olds; for riding ability and jumping without a rider as 4-year-olds; and for jumping and dressage with rider, plus a veterinary examination, as $4\frac{1}{2}$-year-olds. During these tests temperament, character, constitution, fodder intake, fodder utilization, willingness to work, riding ability, jumping ability, working style and general efficiency are marked and each horse is given a 'training score'.

Height   15.2 to 16.2 hands.

Colour   Any solid colour.

Conformation   Varies, but all horses have substance. The heads are intelligent, with width between the eyes. The neck is a good shape and is harmoniously attached to a strong body which is usually broad and deep. The hindquarters are powerfully built, but they can be a little flat.

Uses   Some are outstanding show jumpers and dressage horses, and others are used for harness work, eventing, and general riding.

EQUINE SPECIES

Within the equine family are three types – horse, ass and zebra. These species cannot interbreed. All the breeds in the preceding pages belong to the horse species. The zebra and ass species are discussed below.

Ass (Donkey)

The domesticated ass (or donkey), friendly but stubborn, is familiar throughout the world. Although there are local variations, it is generally slaty grey in colour and averages 10 to 11 hands in height. It has a thick, coarse coat, big head, flat withers, little box-like feet and black dorsal and shoulder stripes. These stripes, which form a cross on the back, are traditionally supposed to date from the first Palm Sunday when Christ rode into Jerusalem on an ass. The donkey is proverbially, and in fact, a very long-lived animal.

In India there are two types of domesticated donkey: the small grey, which averages 8 hands and is the usual dark grey colour with black markings; and the large white, averaging 11 hands. *The wild ass* exists as two distinct types, in Africa and Asia respectively. The African ass, from which the domesticated breeds are derived, is very rare, living in small herds in Nubia, eastern Sudan and Somalia. Grey in colour, except for a white belly, it has large ears and small narrow hooves, and its voice emits the familiar bray. Fast and sure-footed, it is much larger than the domesticated 'Neddy'.

The onager of Asia (*Equus hemionus onager*) is more horse-like, has smaller ears and is sandy or dun in colour. One distinct strain, the Kiang, is found in the Tibetan highlands. The general body colouring is sandy or light chestnut with a black dorsal stripe and tail tuft, while the muzzle, under-neck, belly, legs and back of the thighs are creamy-white. The colour becomes darker during winter, when the coat is long and thick. The Kiang is a powerfully-built animal ranging in height from 12 to 13 hands. It lives in small herds, is very fast for its size and is an exceptionally strong swimmer.

Various local strains of *hemionus*, rather smaller and more lightly built, are found in the desert regions of northwest India, Iran (onager), Tartary and Mongolia (dziggetai). The race indigenous to Syria, which must have been the wild ass of the Bible, is now extinct.

Zebra

The term 'Zebra' is a word of Amharic (Ethiopian) origin meaning 'striped'. It is not the designation given to a breed of the horse family but a descriptive name that applies to three distinct and quite unrelated sub-species of *equus*, that have retained the stripes said to have characterized other members of the horse family in the past. Vestiges of these stripes remain in duns, in certain primitive pony breeds and in some species of the wild ass, eg, the onager and the kiang.

From time immemorial the Zebra, unlike its cousin the horse (*Equus Caballus*), has inhabited only the African continent where it is found from Ethiopia to the Cape, excluding the North African coast. There are a number of local varieties named after the men who discovered them – Burchell, Hartman, Grant, and so on, but each is a member of one or other of three separate species: Grevy's Zebra, the Mountain Zebra and the Quagga.

Grevy's Zebra is the largest of the sub-species, averaging about 13 hands. Its chief distinguishing marks are its long, expanded and round-topped ears, and the pattern of its stripes. These are regular, of uniform size, and change from vertical over the flanks to almost horizontal at the head and hindquarters. The neck stripes are broader than those on the body. The longitudinal spinal stripe broadens out considerably on the croup. Another distinctive characteristic is the sound of its bray. It lives on the open, scrub-covered plains in the lowlands of Ethiopia and northern Kenya.

The Mountain Zebra has its habitat in the mountains of the Cape Province of South Africa, in Botswana, and in Southwest Africa (Namibia). It differs from Grevy's Zebra in having more pointed and ass-like ears, a lighter, more breedy-looking head and a dewlap upon the throat. The stripes are very similar to those of Grevy's Zebra, except that those on the hindquarters are very broad, and curve more gradually from vertical on the flanks to horizontal on the hindquarters and thighs. This animal is the smallest of the three species, averaging about 10 hands. It has not been heard to bray, in fact as far as is known it is quite silent.

The Quagga was at one time found in east and northeast Africa (excluding Egypt). It is very like the Mountain Zebra in appearance, but with even more sweeping patterns of broad stripes curving from flanks to hindquarters. It used also to inhabit South Africa and was first discovered there but, for some unexplained reason, south of the Zambesi it lost most of its stripes, having none on the legs and hindquarters below the tail and only faint ones on the flanks; but this strain is now extinct. It acquired its name from its very distinctive voice, rather like the repetition of three syllables, 'qua-ha-ha', which led the Hotentots to call it the 'Khoua khoua', from which the Boers evolved the word 'Quagga'.

In general, all the Zebra species are very similar to asses in appearance, with stocky bodies, heavy heads, very thick necks, straight shoulders and box-like hooves. Although a few people have succeeded at various times in putting odd specimens to drive between shafts, zebras have rarely proved amenable to domestication and training. The animal is unco-operative and takes most unkindly to any form of tuition.

At one time zebras, especially the Mountain species, were in grave danger of extinction, but these interesting and attractive members of the horse family are now strictly protected.

The zebra's fantastic markings are a marvellous camouflage in its natural surroundings, and it is in the man-made environment of a zoo that their strange patterns can best be examined.

BREEDS OF THE WORLD

Listed under country of origin

ALGERIA

Barb   See page 24.

ARGENTINA

Criollo   See page 44.

Falabella   *Average height* 7 hands. *Colour* Most. *Features* They are the world's smallest horses and are used as pets, and in harness. *Origins* The Falabella family have developed this breed in the country outside Buenos Aires during the past hundred years, basing it on the Shetland Pony, which was developed downwards by in-breeding and crossing with the smallest possible animals.

AUSTRALIA

Australian Pony   *Average height* 13 hands. *Colour* Most. *Features* Used as children's ponies. *Origins* This pony is the result of crossing imported stock – Welsh, Exmoor, Thoroughbred, Shetland and Arab.

Australian Stock Horse (Waler)   *Average height* 14.2 to 16 hands. *Colour* Most. *Features* These vary as this national collective name covers a number of types. Originally they were the horses of graziers and stockmen, and so were agile and tough, with great powers of endurance. They became very famous as cavalry horses, particularly in the years between Waterloo and the Crimean War. Today they are used for rodeo work, on the farms, for general riding and for competitions. *Origins* The first horses in Australia arrived in 1795 from the Cape and Chile. This stock was Dutch and Spanish with Arab and Barb background. More Arab and some English Thoroughbred were added.

Brumby   *Height* and *colour* vary. *Features* This is the wild horse of Australia, evolved when horses turned loose in the last century multiplied in the bush. With in-breeding the quality was not high, and during this century numbers grew so large that they had to be culled. Few now survive. *Origins* All types of imported horses.

AUSTRIA

Austrian Warm-Blood *Average height* 16.1 hands. *Colour* Most. *Features* a new breed which is being developed from other European warm-bloods to be used for riding and competitions.
Hafflinger See page 72.
Lipizzaner See page 96.
Noriker (South German Cold-Blood) *Average height* 16.1 hands. *Colour* Chestnut and bay; sometimes spotted. *Features* Today based around Salzburg in Austria and in Upper and Lower Bavaria in Germany, they have been popular in both countries since the 8th century. Two hundred years ago the distinctive spots were typical of the breed, but today with varied cross-breeding they are rarer. This strong, broad horse with short legs is sure-footed yet active. It is used in agriculture, for mountain work and by the army. *Origins* They were originally bred in the Roman province of Noricum (eastern Alps). The German version, the South German Cold-Blood, has been cross-bred with Norfolk Trotter, Norman, Cleveland, Holstein, Oldenburg, Thoroughbred and Arab over the past two hundred years.

BELGIUM

Ardennes (Ardennais) See page 22.
Belgian Half-Blood *Average height* 16 hands. *Colour* Most. *Features* Developed mainly from French stock, but with some German and Dutch imports, this is becoming an increasingly popular riding and competition horse.
Brabant (Belgian Heavy Draught) See page 28.

BRAZIL

Campolino *Average height* 15 hands. *Colour* Grey, sorrel, roan, bay. *Features* Conformation similar to the Mangalarga but with more substance. Used for light draught work. *Origins* Andalusian and Crioulo.
Crioulo *Average height* 15 hands. *Colour* Dun, with dark points, dorsal stripe and dark snip; roan; sorrel. *Features* Tough, wiry horses with longish necks and high-set tails. Used for riding and herding. *Origins* Criollo and Altér Real.
Mangalarga *Average height* 15 hands. *Colour* Grey, sorrel, roan, bay. *Features* A little lighter than the Criollo. They have an unusual gait called the 'marcha' which is between a trot and

a canter. Used for riding and ranch work. *Origins* Crioulo, Altér Real and Andalusian.

BULGARIA

Danubian *Average height* 15.2 hands. *Colour* Black, dark chestnut. *Features* A compact, deep horse with high-set tail. It is strong and can be used for light draught work and riding. *Origins* Based on the Nonius, it has been up-graded by use of the Anglo-Arab and Thoroughbred.

East Bulgarian *Average height* 16 hands. *Colour* Usually chestnut or black. *Features* Versatile, tough, and a good mover. It has good conformation and is used for riding, competitions and even steeplechasing. *Origins* Its development began at the Kaiuk farm in the late 19th century when Anglo-Arabs, cross-bred English mares, and native Arabian mares were used. Selective breeding has continued since then.

Pleven *Average height* 15.3 hands. *Colour* Most. *Features* Arabian type, harmoniously proportioned and athletic. Used successfully in competitions and for general riding. *Origins* Anglo-Arab and Arab, of native Russian and Hungarian stock. Recently the Thoroughbred has been used to improve it as a competition horse.

BURMA

Burmese (Shan) *Average height* 13 hands. *Colour* Most. *Features* It is a larger version of the Manipur bred by the hill tribes of the Shan States, and is believed to be closely related to the Mongolian breed. It is deep, short-coupled, with sloping croup, and is used as a general work pony. *Origins* Mongolian pony.

CANADA

Sable Island *Average height* 14 hands. *Colour* Most, but chestnut predominates. *Features* Tough wiry ponies which graze in small herds on Sable Island off the coast of Nova Scotia. They are used as harness and riding ponies, especially by the lighthouse keepers. *Origins* Foundation stock were New England ponies brought to the Island in the early 18th century.

CHINA

China Pony *Average height* 14 hands. *Colour* Most. *Features* Fast pony used for riding and racing. *Origins* Mongolians crossed with Arabs and Thoroughbreds.

Mongolian   See page 101.
Mongolian Wild Horse (Przevalski's Horse; Asian Wild Horse)   See page 100.

CZECHOSLOVAKIA

Kladruber   See page 88.
Lipizzaner   See page 96.

DENMARK

Danish Warm-Blood   *Average height* 16 hands. *Colour* Most solid colours. *Features* A variety of types, but all tending to have an excellent, tractable temperament. They have good movement and are athletic. Used for riding, and have achieved excellent results in international competitions. *Origins* Developed since the early 1960s by using selected breeding stock, proved through testing. The main breeds used have been Hanoverian, Oldenburg, Swedish, Trakehner and Thoroughbred.
Frederiksborg   *Average height* 15.3 hands. *Colour* Chestnut. *Features* A strong, plain horse with active movement and good temperament. Originally bred at the royal stud of Frederiksborg, it was a very popular breed during the 17th, 18th and early 19th centuries. Used for harness and riding work, but few good examples are found today. *Origins* Indigenous Danish, plus Andalusian and Neapolitan.
Jutland   See page 86.
Knabstrup   See page 90.

FINLAND

Finnish   *Average height* 15.2 hands. *Colour* Chestnut, bay, brown. *Features* This cold-blood tends to have a short neck with an upright shoulder, but with a deep body and strong legs. Tough and fast, it is used in agriculture, for timber hauling, and in trotting races. *Origins* With the reduced demand for horses, the two original Finnish breeds, the Finnish Universal (an indigenous forest pony) and the Finnish Draught, were merged to produce the Finnish.

FRANCE

Anglo-Arab   See page 14.
Ardennes (Ardennais)   See page 22.
Basque   *Average height* 13 hands. *Colour* Most. *Features* Primitive type with slightly concave head, short neck and long

back. It is tough and still roams wild in the Pyrennees and Atlantic cantons. It is used for riding and at one time was a pit pony. *Origins* Unknown.

Boulonnais   See page 26.

Breton   See page 30.

Camargue (Camarguais)   See page 34.

Comtois   *Average height* 15.1 hands. *Colour* Bay, chestnut. *Features* This cold-blood with its straight neck and long, straight back is active and sure-footed; it is used by the Army and by farmers. *Origins* It is an ancient breed, but Percheron, Norman, Boulonnais and Ardennais blood have been added.

French Trotter   See page 58.

Landais   *Average height* 13.2 hands. *Colour* Dark tones. *Features* Shape varies, but it usually has a fine frame with an Arab-like head. It is used for riding and driving. *Origins* Native stock plus Arab.

Percheron   See page 116.

Poitevin   *Average height* 16.3 hands. *Colour* Dun. *Features* A large head and long body; a docile nature. A major use is putting mares to jackasses to produce mules. *Origins* They come from the flatlands of northern Europe and have Norwegian, Danish and Dutch blood.

Selle Français   See page 128.

GERMAN DEMOCRATIC REPUBLIC (EAST GERMANY)

East Friesian   *Average height* 16.1 hands. *Colour* Most solid colours. *Features* A strong horse which is a lighter and more elegant version of the Oldenburg. It is used for riding and harness work. *Origins* Based on the Oldenburg, but since the partition of Germany some Arab blood has been added.

Edle Warm-Blood   *Average height* 16.1 hands. *Colour* Chestnut most common. *Features* Active straight movers with substance. *Origins* Hanoverian and Trakehner foundations used to develop this new breed.

Mecklenburg   *Average height* 16 hands. *Colour* Most solid colours. *Features* Similar to the Hanoverian but a little smaller. It is used for general riding, for competitions, and by the army. *Origins* Originally a cold-blood horse, it has a history similar to that of the Hanoverian. It has been lightened over the centuries and recently a good deal of Hanoverian blood has been used.

FEDERAL REPUBLIC OF GERMANY (WEST GERMANY)

Baden-Würtemburg *Average height* 16 hands. *Colour* Most solid colours. *Features* Athletic horse used for competitions and general riding. *Origins* The Wurtemburg – a cob type – was bred in south-west Germany for centuries. The Trakehner was used to upgrade it into a riding horse. The main centre for this breeding was the Marbach stud.

Bavarian *Average height* 16 hands. *Colour* Most. *Features* A medium-sized, deep and broad horse with good temperament and athletic ability. Used for riding. *Origins* Rottaler (a battle charger), Thoroughbred, Cleveland, Norman, and other German breeds.

Dülmen *Average height* 12.3 hands. *Colour* Most are black, brown or dun. *Features* These ponies are becoming rarer, but most live semi-wild on a reserve in Westphalia. Owned by the Duke of Croy, they have been subjected to cross-breeding with British and Polish ponies.

Hanoverian See page 74.

Hessen and Rheinlander Pfalz *Average height* 16 hands. *Colour* Most. *Features* A good-moving strong horse with even temperament. Used for riding. *Origins* Based on other regional German breeds.

Holstein See page 78.

Oldenburg See page 110.

Rhenish-German Heavy Draught *Average height* 16.2 hands. *Colour* Chestnut, roan with flaxen mane and tail, or red roan with black mane and tail. *Features* A heavy, strong, compact horse used for draught work. *Origins* Ardennais and local heavy horses.

Rhineland *Average height* 16.1 hands. *Colour* Most. *Features* Another of Germany's regional breeds suitable for riding and competitions. *Origins* Based on the Westphalian.

Schleswig See page 126.

South-German Cold-Blood *Average height* 16.1 hands. *Colour* Most. *Features* This is the German version of Austria's Noriker. It is used by the farmers and previously by the army especially in the mountains. *Origins* In the Bavarian mountains Norman, Cleveland, Holstein, Hungarian, Clydesdale and Oldenburg blood has been added to Noriker foundation stock.

Trakehner See page 154.

Westphalian See page 162.

GREECE

Peneia   *Average height* Ranges from 10 to 14 hands. *Colour* Most. *Features* A tough, hardy pony with Oriental characteristics. Used for pack work and on farms. *Origins* Oriental and native stock.

Pindos   *Average height* 12.2 hands. *Colour* Grey and dark colours. *Features* A fine but tough pony used for riding and for farm work. The mares are used for breeding mules. *Origins* Ancient. Some oriental blood has been added.

Skyros   *Average height* 10 hands. *Colour* Dun, brown, grey. *Features* Lacks substance and often has cow hocks with a rather straight shoulder. Bred on the Island of Skyros, where it is used for all types of work – on farms, for transport, riding and carrying water. *Origins* Ancient, it is thought to have been of Tarpan stock.

HUNGARY

Furioso   See page 81.

Gidran   See page 81.

Hungarian Half-bred   See page 80.

Murakosi   *Average height* 16 hands. *Colour* Chestnut with flaxen mane and tail. *Features* This strong cold-blood tends to have a dipped back with well-rounded hindquarters. There is little feather and it is an active type used in agriculture and for general draught work. *Origins* The native mares (Mur-Insulan) were crossed with Oriental, Percheron and Ardennais.

Kisber   See page 81.

Mezohegyes   See page 81.

Shagya   See page 130.

ICELAND

Icelandic Pony   See page 82.

INDIA

Bhutia   See Spiti and Bhutia.

Kathiawari and Marwari   *Average height* 14.2 hands. *Colour* Chestnut, brown, bay, grey, piebald and skewbald with some creams. *Features* These two wiry, narrow country-breds originated in Kathiawar and the former Rajputana, in northwest India, but are now found over most of the subcontinent. Their conformation is not good, but they have tremendous powers of endurance, and help the peasants in their primitive agriculture.

Origins Both are said to have developed from a shipload of Arab horses wrecked on the west coast of India. They ran wild, and cross-bred with the indigenous country-bred ponies, to produce these two tough breeds.

Manipur *Average height* 12 hands. *Colour* Most. *Features* Sturdy and sure-footed, they are quick and manoeuvrable. Used for polo when the game became popular with the British in the last century. They have also been valued by the army for transport purposes. *Origins* There is evidence of their existence as early as the 7th century AD in the State of Manipur in Assam. Appearance suggests that they developed from the Mongolian pony and Arabs.

Marwari See Kathiawari and Marwari.

Spiti and Bhutia *Average height* Spiti 12 hands; Bhutia 13.1 hands. *Colour* Grey. *Features* Bred in and around the Himalayas, these two regional breeds of pony have been the major source of transport in difficult areas. They are strong enough to carry heavy men or large packs. They are both thick-set, short-coupled, tough and very sure-footed. The Spiti is bred by a tribe of high-caste Hindus called the Kanyats, and considerable in-breeding is practised to keep down the size. *Origins* Unproven, but probably from the Mongolian pony.

INDONESIA

Bali *Average height* 12.2 hands. *Colour* Dun with dorsal stripe and dark points. *Features* A sturdy, frugal, strong pony, used for riding and pack work. *Origins* Mongolian and Asiatic Wild Horse.

Batak *Average height* 12.2 hands. *Colour* Most. *Features* A rather elegant pony, strong and with a good temperament. Used for agriculture and transport. *Origins* Arab and indigenous ponies.

Java *Average height* 12.1 hands. *Colour* Most. *Features* Tough, wiry frame but poor conformation. They are famous as ponies for pulling 'sados' (two-wheeled cabs). *Origins* Tarpan and Mongolian Wild Horse.

Sandalwood *Average height* 12.3 hands. *Colour* Most, but the coat is usually burnished. *Features* Lighter, more refined and faster than most other types of Indonesian pony. Used for bareback racing and general work. *Origins* Arab and native ponies.

Sumba *Average height* 12.2 hands. *Colour* Dun with dorsal stripe and dark mane and tail. *Features* A primitive type of pony famous for its unusual 'dancing' steps. Used for general work. *Origins* Mongolian.

Timor   *Average height* 11.1 hands. *Colour* Most. *Features* A sturdy, agile pony with a good temperament and turn of speed, used for herding and general riding. *Origins* Mongolian Wild Horse and probably some Tarpan.

IRAN

Caspian   See page 36.

Pahlavan   *Average height* 15.3 hands. *Colour* Solid colours. *Features* A strong, elegant riding horse used for racing and jumping. Selectively developed as a breed in the 1950s at the royal stud. *Origins* Thoroughbred, Plateau Persian, and Arab.

Persian Arab   See page 19.

Plateau Persian   *Average height* 15 hands. *Colour* Grey, bay, chestnut. *Features* Strong, sure-footed riding horses with good action. Arab features. *Origins* Regional breeds of Iran (Jaf, Arab strains, Basseri, Darashouri, Shirazi, Bakhtiari) were amalgamated to establish this new breed.

Turkoman   *Average height* 15.1 hands. *Colour* Most solid colours. *Features* Narrow but tough, with free action, speed and endurance. Bred for hundreds of years on Turkoman steppes. Those in Russia, known as Akhal-Teké (see page 8) and Iomud (Yomud), have long been used as foundation stock for other breeds. Famous as cavalry horses, and also used for racing and general riding. The Iranian strain of Turkoman is also known as the Tchenaran. *Origins* Said to have developed from horses left by raiding Mongols and from animals bred by Scythians around 100 AD.

REPUBLIC OF IRELAND

Connemara   See page 42.

Irish Draught   See page 84.

Irish Horse   *Average height* 16.1 hands. *Colour* Most. *Features* Shape varies, but they are strong athletic horses with a good temperament, used for hunting, riding and competitions. *Origins* Since the 1970s the Irish have selected their breeding stock and registered its produce as Irish Horses. The most important blood is Irish Draught, Thoroughbred and some Connemara.

ITALY

Avelignese *Average height* 14 hands. *Colour* Chestnut, with flaxen mane and tail. *Features* This is Italy's version of the Hafflinger, being similar in physique and in uses, ie, for work in the mountains and on farms. It is a little heavier. *Origins* Similar to those of the Hafflinger, but probably less Oriental blood has been added.

Calabrese *Average height* 16 hands. *Colour* Most solid colours. *Features* A middleweight, short-coupled riding horse. *Origins* Based on the Neapolitan.

Italian Heavy Draught *Average height* 15.2 hands. *Colour* Sorrel, roan. *Features* Long but elegant head, short neck, flat back and powerful hindquarters. It is fast, strong and has a kind temperament. Used in agriculture and for its meat. *Origins* Based on the Breton.

Italian Saddle Horse *Average height* 16 hands. *Colour* Most solid colours. *Features* There is still great variety of types registered, as this breed group is in the early stages of development. *Origins* The regional breeds like the Sicilian and Sardinian Anglo Arab, the Salernos, the Maremannos and the Sanfrantellanos have been merged and crossed with warmbloods from France, Germany and Ireland.

Murghese *Average height* 15.2 hands. *Colour* Sorrel. *Features* A heavier version of the Oriental horse. It is versatile and used both by farmers and general riders. *Origins* Oriental.

Salerno *Average height* 16 hands. *Colour* Solid colours. *Features* Harmoniously proportioned. Popular for riding, and used by the army. *Origins* Based on the Neapolitan.

JAPAN

Hokkaido *Average height* 13 hands. *Colour* Dun is the most usual, with dorsal stripe and with black point. *Features* Compact and tough, it is very closely related and similar to the Mongolian. *Origins* Mongolian.

MEXICO

Galiceño *Average height* 12.2 hands. *Colour* Bay, black sorrel, dun, grey. *Features* A short-coupled, narrow pony with a straightish shoulder and back. It is versatile, intelligent and has a natural running walk. Used for ranch work, transport and competitions. *Origins* Based on Garranos brought to the New World from Portugal.

MOROCCO

Barb   See page 24.

NETHERLANDS

Dutch Draught   See page 52.
Dutch Warm-Blood   *Average height* 16.1 hands. *Colour* Most. *Features* An athletic kind horse which has excelled as a competition horse since the 1970s. *Origins* The native heavier Dutch breeds of Groningen and Gelderland were selectively bred to Thoroughbreds, Arabs, French and German warm-bloods.
Friesian   See page 60.
Gelderland   See page 62.
Groningen   See page 66.

NORWAY

Dole   *Average height* 15 hands. *Colour* Black, brown, bay. *Features* There are two types: the draught, which is similar to the British Fell, and the pony type with its rather straight shoulder, deep body, round hindquarters and short legs. Tough and versatile, they are used under saddle and in harness on farms and for pleasure. *Origins* Danish cold-blood, Thoroughbred, Trotter.
Dole Trotter   *Average height* 15 hands. *Colour* Black, brown, bay. *Features* A lighter version of the Dole, used in trotting races. *Origins* Dole plus Trotter.
Norwegian-Fjord   See page 108.

PERU

Peruvian Stepping Horse (Peruvian Paso)   See page 118.

POLAND

Huçul   See page 92.
Konik   See page 92.
Malapolski   *Average height* 16 hands. *Colour* Bay, grey chestnut and black. *Features* A strong all-round horse which is used by farmers and riders. *Origins* Local primitive stock was crossed with Arabs and Thoroughbreds. Shagyas Furiosos, Gidrans and Lipizzaners were also used.
Polish Arab   See page 19.
Polish Draught   *Average height* Wide range. *Colour* Most. *Features* Regional breeds of draught horses have been developed

in Poland to suit local demands. The largest is the Sztum to which the Løwicz is similar but lighter. The Sokolka has Ardennes as foundation blood as does the Garvolin. Smaller than these is the Lidzbark but the smallest of all is the Kopczuk Podlaski.

Sokolka   *Average height* 15.2 hands. *Colour* Chestnut, brown, grey. *Features* This strong horse has a short straight back, short legs with little feather and large round feet. Economical to keep and docile in temperament, it is ideal for farm work. *Origins* Breton, Ardennais, Belgian, Anglo-Norman.

Tarpan   See page 142.

Wielkopolski   *Average height* 16 hands. *Colour* Chestnut, bay. *Features* A harmoniously proportioned, athletic horse, used for general riding, harness work and competitions. *Origins* Amalgamation of Poland's two major breeds of saddle horse, the Masuren (based on Trakehner blood) and the Poznan (based on Konik, Thoroughbred, Hanoverian and Trakehner blood).

PORTUGAL

Altér Real   See page 10.

Garrano (Minho)   *Average height* 11 hands. *Colour* Dark chestnut. *Features* A light pony with good conformation and a very full mane and tail. It is used for riding and pack work. *Origins* Very ancient. Some Arab blood has been added.

Lusitano   See page 98.

Sorraia   *Average height* 13 hands. *Colour* Dun with dorsal stripe and stripes on legs. *Features* A primitive type, tough and frugal. It still runs wild, and has probably done so since Neolithic times, on the plains between the rivers of Sor and Raia. *Origins* As some of the ponies have a Tarpan-like face, it is likely that they are of Tarpan ancestry.

PUERTO RICO

Paso Fino   *Average height* 14.3 hands. *Colour* Most. *Features* A powerful horse with Arab features. Known for its special four-beat gaits, ranging from the slow 'paso fino' through the 'paso corto' to the fastest, the 'paso largo'. *Origins* Spanish horses.

SOUTH AFRICA

Basuto   *Average height* 14.2 hands. *Colour* Chestnut, bay, brown, grey. *Features* Small, thick-set, short legs, longish back and very hard hooves. Quality head. One of the most fearless and sure-footed ponies in the world, with great powers of endurance. Used for trekking, pack work, polo, racing and general riding. *Origins* Arabs and Barbs, from which the Cape horse was established in the 17th century, plus up-grading by Arab, Barb, Persian and Thoroughbred in the 19th century.

SPAIN

Andalusian See page 12.

Hispano *Average height* 16 hands. *Colour* Bay, chestnut, grey. *Features* A bold, versatile horse used for eventing, jumping, dressage and military work. *Origins* It is the Spanish Anglo-Arab, developed by crossing Spanish-Arabian mares with Thoroughbreds.

(MAJORCA)
Balearic *Average height* 14 hands. *Colour* Bay, brown. *Features* The head is fine but the nose is usually Roman. The body is light but tough. It usually stands with its ears drawn back. It is docile and is used for harness and farm work. *Origins* Balearics are of ancient origin and are said to look like the horses on early Greek coins. Sadly this breed is close to extinction.

SWEDEN

Ardennes (Ardennais) See page 22.

Gotland (Russ) See page 64.

North Swedish *Average height* 15.2 hands. *Colour* Most solid colours. *Features* A robust type which is a fast trotter and is still used for log hauling. *Origins* It is closely related to the Dole from Norway.

Swedish Warm-Blood See page 140.

SWITZERLAND

Freiberger (Franches-Montagnes) *Average height* 15.3 to 16.1 hands. *Colour* Originally mainly chestnut, now also grey and blue-roan. *Features* Compact, elegant yet sturdy horses, with great stamina, used for light draught, agriculture and riding. *Origins* They came from the Jura mountains but are now mainly bred at Avenches near Lausanne. During this century the stock has been lightened with Arab (largely Shagya) blood.

Swiss Warm-Blood *Average height* 16.1 hands. *Colour* Most solid colours. *Features* A powerful horse with good action and kind temperament, used for riding, competitions, and harness work. *Origins* Developed since the 1960s from Swedish, German, Anglo-Norman and Thoroughbred stock, to provide riding horses. This Swiss stock used was the Einsiedelner, a breed which originated in the eleventh century thanks to the monks at Einsiedeln.

TIBET

Native Tibetan (Nanfan) *Average height* 12.2 hands. *Colour* Usually white coat with unpigmented skin. *Features* A tough, sure-footed pony used in the Tibetan regions of the Himalayas. An energetic, fast walker, it is used for agricultural and pack work. *Origins* Since it closely resembles the Spiti and Bhutia from India, its origin must be similar, ie, the Mongolian pony.

TURKEY

Karacabey *Average height* 16 hands. *Colour* Any solid colour. *Features* A tough well-made horse, used for light draught work, especially in agriculture, and as a cavalry horse. *Origins* Native mares and Nonius.

UNITED KINGDOM

British Warm-Blood *Average height* 16.1 hands. *Colour* Most. *Features* They are bred for their sensible temperament, good movement and sound conformation. The actual shape varies considerably. They are good saddle and harness horses and have done well in dressage and show jumping. *Origins* Since the late 1970s breeding stock has been inspected and graded, based on Continental stock which is crossed with further graded Continental stock or Thoroughbreds.

Suffolk   See page 138.
Thoroughbred   See page 148.
Welsh Cob   See page 158.
Welsh Mountain   See page 160.
Welsh Pony (Section B)   See page 160.
Welsh Pony (Cob Type) (Section C)   See page 158.

USA

Albino   *Average height* Varies. *Colour* Snow white; pink skin; pale blue or dark brown eyes. *Features* A colour type, not a breed, it has been developed since 1937 by the American Albino Horse Club. The alleged foundation sire was 'Old King' (1906), possibly of Arabian-Morgan stock. By careful selection, any type of Albino can be developed, for riding or for draught. Naturally, however, many are used for ceremonial purposes and in the circus ring.
Appaloosa   See page 16.
Missouri Foxtrotter   *Average height* 15 hands. *Colour* Any. *Features* Kind, docile horse with a special gait called the fox trot. In this the horse walks in front and trots behind which gives a fast comfortable ride. It is popular for trail riding and showing. *Origins* Developed in Missouri in the nineteenth century from Arabs, Morgans and Southern Plantation Horses. Standardbred, Saddlebred and Tennessee Walker blood was added later.
Morgan   See page 102.
Mustang   See page 104.
Palomino   See page 114.
Pinto   See page 120.
Pony of Americas   *Average height* 12.1 hands. *Colour* Appaloosa patterning. *Features* Arab-like head, short back. A broad pony used by children for riding, trail riding and competitions. *Origins* In 1956 Leslie Boomhower in Iowa crossed a Shetland stallion with an Appaloosa mare to produce a miniature Appaloosa colt called 'Black Hand'. This stallion became the foundation of a breed which has quickly multiplied. Qualification for registration is height (11.2 to 13 hands) and colouring, which must be an Appaloosa pattern.
Quarter Horse   See page 122.
Saddlebred   See page 124.
Standardbred   See page 136.
Tennessee Walking Horse   See page 144.

USSR

Akhal-Teké   See page 8.

Altai   *Average height* 13 hands. *Colour* Chestnut, bay and black are most common. *Features* Primitive type with a largish head and long back. *Origins* Similar to the Mongolian and Huçul.

Bashkirsky   *Average height* 13.2 hands. *Colour* Bay, dun, chestnut. *Features* This thick-set pony with its long back, low-set tail and short legs is very tough and has a good temperament. Used for riding and for pulling sleighs; the mares are milked for 'kumiss', a medicinal and alcoholic drink. *Origins* The original native pony was improved by crossing with Budyonny, Don and Orlov Trotter.

Budyonny   See page 32.

Buryat   *Average height* 13.2 hands. *Colour* Light brown with black mane and tail, chestnut, bay and grey. *Features* Large in the body but short in the legs with good bone, it is quite fast and used both for driving and riding in Siberia. *Origins* An old breed which has been influenced by the Mongolian.

Don   See page 50.

Estonian   *Average height* 14 hands. *Colour* Usually brown, bay or chestnut. *Features* Docile but energetic, it has a short neck and back but a long croup with rather fine boned legs. *Origins* It has been bred for more than 900 years in Estonia.

Iomud   *Average height* 14.3 hands. *Colour* Grey, chestnut, bay. *Features* Similar to the Akhal-Teké, but more compact. Less fast, it is used for distance and general riding, and by the cavalry. *Origins* Like the Akhal-Teké, it is an old breed, derived from the Turkoman.

Kabardin   *Average height* 15 hands. *Colour* Bay, black. *Features* This stout horse with short legs and long, straight back has long been bred and used in the mountain regions of the northern Caucasus. A good pack or riding horse, it competes in the local equestrian games. *Origins* Thought to be the result of crossing Arabs and Karabakhs with eastern steppe horses.

Karabair   *Average height* 15.1 hands. *Colour* Bay, chestnut, grey. *Features* Ancient mountain breed from Uzbekistan. Three types exist: the finest is the riding horse, the strongest is the harness horse; and between them is the utility version used for saddle and harness work. They have an Oriental look, but with a straight face. They are tough and used for farm work and general riding. *Origins* Arab and Mongolian.

183

Karabakh   *Average height* 14.1 hands. *Colour* Chestnut, bay, grey, dun, all with golden sheen to coats. *Features* An Arabian type, mentioned as early as the 4th century AD. It was popular in the past for riding, and was used to improve such breeds as the Don and Kabardin. *Origins* Persian, Turkoman.

Kazakh   *Average height* 13 hands. *Colour* Bay, chestnut, grey. *Features* Similar to the Mongolian, it can be differentiated into two types, the heavier Dzhabye and the lighter Adayevsky. It is tough, has great powers of endurance, and has been used by the cavalry especially when crossed with the Don or Akhal-Teké. The mares provide milk used for 'kumiss' and some are used for herding livestock. *Origins* Mongolian.

Kushum   *Average height* 15.2 hands. *Colour* Usually bay or chestnut. *Features* This new breed was developed in the 1930s mainly to supply the meat market. It is a strong horse with much stamina. *Origins* Kazakhs, Thoroughbreds, Arabs and Dons were the foundation stock.

Kustanair   *Average height* 15.1 hands. *Colour* Chestnut or bay. *Features* A strong lightly built horse, it is tough enough to survive the weather conditions of Kazakhstan. *Origins* Kazakh mares were upgraded firstly by use of Don and Strelets stallions, then Thoroughbreds.

Latvian   See page 94.

Lithuanian Heavy Draught   *Average height* 15.1 hands. *Colour* Usually chestnut. *Features* Large head with a strong muscular body, it is tough and has a long life. It is used in agriculture and for meat. *Origins* Ardennes were bred to the Zhmuds at the beginning of this century.

Lokai   *Average height* 14.3 hands. *Colour* Grey, bay, chestnut, often with a golden tint. *Features* A mountain pack and riding horse, in particular in Tadzhikstan. It is a sturdy, tough, sure-footed pony with great powers of endurance. Like the Karabair it was developed by the Uzbeks. In the 16th century the Lokai tribe had small ponies which were later improved by cross-breeding with the Iomud, Karabair and with Arab stock.

Novokirghiz   *Average height* 15 hands. *Colour* Bay, chestnut or grey. *Features* Muscular longish body, legs short. Used in the mountains for riding, harness, transport and sport. It is also swift and used for long-distance racing. Its milk is used to make 'kumiss'. *Origins* Developed in Kirgiz from ancient Kirgiz stock (Mongolian origins) crossed with Don and Thoroughbred.

Orlov Trotter   See page 112.

Russian Heavy Draught *Average height* 14.3 hands. *Colour* Chestnut, bay, roan. *Features* One of the smallest cold-bloods, very thick-set, strong and active. Used by farmers and for transport. *Origins* Local Ukraine cart mares crossed with Belgians, Swedish Ardennes and Orlov Trotters.

Russian Trotter *Average height* 15.3 hands. *Colour* Black, bay, chestnut. *Features* Fast trotter. *Origins* Orlovs crossed with Standardbreds.

Soviet Heavy Draught *Average height* 15.2 hands. *Colour* Most are chestnut or roan. *Features* A docile tough horse with muscular broad body. It is a very popular draught horse in western Russia. *Origins* Belgian Heavy Draughts were imported last century and crossed with local mares to start this breed.

Tersky See page 146.

Toric See page 152.

Ukrainian Riding Horse *Average height* 16 hands. *Colour* Usually bay, chestnut or black. *Features* This new breed group is a very popular sports horse and is strong and athletic. *Origins* Developed in the Ukraine from imported Hanoverians, Trakehners, Noniuses, Furiosos and Gidrans which were crossed with local riding horses.

Viatka See page 156.

Vladimir Heavy Draught *Average height* 16 hands. *Colour* Most solid colours. *Features* Strong cold-blood with good conformation. Feather on legs. It is active and used for all types of draught work. *Origins* Established as a breed in 1946, having been developed from Cleveland, Suffolk, Percheron, Shire and Ardennais blood over the previous 50 years.

Zemaituka/Zhmud *Average height* 13.3 hands. *Colour* Usually dun, with light tail and mane, but can be mouse or bay. There is a dorsal stripe. *Features* Compact, sturdy well-made animal, full of latent fire and energy. A tough primitive type native to the wide grasslands of Lithuania. *Origins* The two main strains were the Tartar pony of the steppes (Przevalski or Mongolian Horse) and the Arab, brought by invading Teutonic knights from western Europe.

YUGOSLAVIA

Bosnian *Average height* 12.2 hands. *Colour* Dun, brown, chestnut, grey, black. *Features* Tough, compact mountain pony, similar to the Huçul; used for pack, harness, riding on farms and in the mountains. *Origins* Tarpan, steppe ponies, Eastern blood.

GLOSSARY OF TECHNICAL TERMS

Many of these definitions are based on those given in
Summerhays' Encyclopaedia for Horsemen

Back at the knee   Forelegs which when viewed from the side tend to concavity below the knee.

Barrel   That part of a horse's body encompassed by the ribs.

Bone   Circumference of a foreleg just below the knee.

Cold-blood   The heavy draught-horse breeds.

Colt   A male horse under the age of four.

Concave (dished face)   Where the line of the face tends to be slightly hollowed.

Conformation   The make and shape of a horse.

Cow-hocks   Hocks turned inwards at the points.

Deep through the girth   A horse that is well-ribbed-up, with generous depth of girth behind the elbows (see **Heart room**).

Dishing   A faulty movement of the forefeet which, when in motion, are thrown backwards and in an outward circular movement to the front again.

Dorsal stripe   A stripe running down the neck and along the top of the body, sometimes to the tip of the tail.

Ewe neck   Where the line of the neck from ears to wither is concave.

Face markings   These include: *blaze*, a white marking covering almost the whole forehead between the eyes, and extending down the front of the face across the whole width of the nasal bones; *muzzle markings*, including both lips and extending to the nostrils; *star markings*, appearing on the forehead; *strip markings*, extending down the face and no wider than the flat anterior surface of the nasal bones.

Feather   Hair on all four heels.

Filly   A female horse under the age of four.

Foal   A colt or filly up to the age of 12 months.

Forehand   The head, neck, shoulders, withers and fore-legs.

Glass, chalk, china or wall-eye   A light blue eye, having a preponderance of white.

Heart-room   See also **Deep through the girth**.

Height   The height of a horse is taken from the highest part of the withers in a perpendicular line to the ground. The horse stands so many hands (a hand is 10.16 cm or 4 inches), or so many hands and so many inches high, but today the height is frequently measured in centimetres.

Hot-blood Horses of the desert and their descendants.

Limb markings These include: *coronet markings*, white hair immediately above the hoof; *fetlock markings*, around and below the fetlock joint; *heel markings*, from the back of the pastern to the ergot; *pastern markings*, immediately below the fetlock joint, extending downwards; *sock markings*, reaching about halfway up the cannon bone; *stocking markings*, extending to the knee or the hock.

Mare The female equine animal.

Mealy nose or muzzle Of an oatmeal colour, running well up the muzzle and having no white markings.

Odd-coloured A coat in which there are more than two colours tending to merge into each other.

Over at the knee A forward bend of the knees.

Pacer A horse which, instead of trotting with a diagonal action, moves like a camel, near-fore and hind together, followed by off-fore and hind. The action is also known as **Ambling**, the old English name for a pacer being an **Ambler**.

Piebald A horse having black and white patches.

Pigeon-toes Toes that turn inwards.

Roan colour An admixture of white hair with the body colour, lightening the general effect of the latter. Thus *blue roan* has black or brown as the body colour, *bay* or *red roan* has bay or bay-brown, and *strawberry* or *chestnut roan* has chestnut.

Roman nose A head with a convex front.

Shoulders *Sloping* – running obliquely from the point of the shoulder to the withers. *Straight* – less oblique.

Sickle hocks Hocks which, when looked at from the side have a sickle or crescent-like appearance.

Skewbald A horse with similar markings to those of the piebald, but with colours other than black.

Stallion A horse capable of reproducing the species, also known as 'entire', or a stud – an ungelded horse.

Tied-in below the knee The leg width immediately below the knee is less than the measurement taken lower down towards the fetlock joint. A horse can also be 'tied-in under the hock'.

Toad eye Found only in the Exmoor pony. A mealy rim to both eyelids, and practically encircling the prominent eye.

Wall-eye See **glass eye**.

Warm-blood Most of the saddle and harness horse breeds.

Well-let-down hocks Hocks which are relatively close to the ground, with short cannon bones.

Well-topped A horse that is deep in its girth and has a good strong body above the legs.

INDEX

INDEX